# BILINGUAL EDUCATION

Loreta Medina, *Book Editor*

Daniel Leone, *President*
Bonnie Szumski, *Publisher*
Scott Barbour, *Managing Editor*
Helen Cothran, *Senior Editor*

San Diego • Detroit • New York • San Francisco • Cleveland
New Haven, Conn. • Waterville, Maine • London • Munich

**LIBRARY OF CONGRESS CATALOGING-IN-PUBLICATION DATA**

Bilingual education / Loreta Medina, book editor.
   p. cm. — (At issue)
Includes bibliographical references and index.
ISBN 0-7377-1606-1 (pbk. : alk. paper) —
ISBN 0-7377-1605-3 (lib. bdg. : alk. paper)
   1. Education, Bilingual—Social aspects—United States. I. Medina, Loreta.
II. At issue (San Diego, Calif.)
LC3731.B5517 2003
370.117'5'0973—dc21
                                            2003044863

Printed in the United States of America

# Contents

# Introduction

In the United States, the term *bilingual education* generally refers to programs that provide support to students with limited English proficiency. Some of these programs teach academic subjects in the students' home language (usually Spanish) while also requiring language-minority students to take classes in English as a second language (ESL). Other programs aim to teach English to language-minority students by immersing them in English-only classes. Still others are two-way, or dual-language, programs that aim for fluency in two languages—for example, such a program might simultaneously teach Spanish to English-speaking students and English to Spanish-speaking students. These major approaches have several variations, and districts and schools may use a combination of them.

Thus, when people argue over bilingual education's effectiveness or ineffectiveness, they could be discussing different forms of bilingual education. In public debate, however, *bilingual education* usually refers to transitional bilingual education (TBE), which provides native-language instruction to non-English-speaking students in preparation for their eventual learning of English in mainstream classes. The goal of these programs is to help students become fluent in English.

In the United States, bilingual education in its modern form began in 1968 with Title VII of the Elementary and Secondary Education Act, which provides federal funding to schools to help them meet the needs of children with limited English-speaking ability. Title VII, also called the Bilingual Education Act, was born out of the civil rights movement, which, among other things, sought to strengthen economic, political, and social opportunities for minorities. The Bilingual Education Act, together with the Civil Rights Act of 1964, was expected to help change attitudes toward immigrant groups and ease resistance to ethnic languages.

The Bilingual Education Act resulted in the implementation of TBE programs in more than half the states, particularly in districts and schools that had large immigrant (most often Hispanic) populations. TBE programs, in which students are instructed in their native language before being taught English, revived a trend from the eighteenth and nineteenth centuries, when bilingual education thrived among the early European settlers who sought to have children instructed in their mother tongue. In 1968, however, bilingual education was envisioned as a way to help Spanish-speaking children who had limited or no skills in English and were doing poorly in school.

## Support for bilingual education

Advocates of bilingual education marshal a variety of arguments in its defense. Key supporters of bilingual education—among them academics like Kenji Hakuta of Stanford University, Colin Baker of the University of

Wales, Stephen Krashen of the University of Southern California, and Jim Cummins of the University of Toronto—emphasize the effectiveness of using students' native language as a resource in learning a second language. They maintain that the use of the students' home language helps keep them from falling behind their fellow students while learning English. They claim that the first language serves as a bridge on learning, and that knowledge acquired in one language transfers to the other language. This means that a child who is not fluent in English but is fluent in Spanish will learn English easily because he has already learned the foundational processes in the first language. The "knowledge-transfer" hypothesis rests on the premise that the process of reading is similar across languages, even though the languages and writing systems are different. As professor of education Stephen Krashen, author of *Under Attack: The Case Against Bilingual Education*, explains,

> When schools provide children quality education in their primary language, they give them two things: knowledge and literacy. The *knowledge* that children get through their first language helps make the English they hear and read more comprehensible. *Literacy* developed in the primary language transfers to the second language. The reason is simple: Because we learn by reading, that is, by making sense of what is on the page, it is easier to learn to read in a language we understand. Once we can read in one language, we can read in general.

Notice that Krashen uses the word *quality*; it is a word that practitioners of bilingual education often emphasize. They maintain that the most effective bilingual education programs are two-way bilingual programs. Such programs aim to teach both native speakers of Spanish and native speakers of English, attending the same classes, academic subjects in both languages. The students initially receive 90 percent of instruction in Spanish and 10 percent in English, and then the amount of English increases with each grade. Supporters of these programs point to studies, such as the one by researchers Wayne P. Thomas and Virginia Collier at George Mason University in Fairfax, Virginia, that document the effectiveness of two-way bilingual programs. Thomas and Collier reviewed student records from 1982 to 2000 and found that English-language learners do better academically over the long term if English is introduced slowly instead of being submerged in intensive English instruction in a regular classroom. They conclude that two-way bilingual programs are "the only kinds of programs that fully close the achievement gap between English-language learners and native English-speakers over the long term."

Most advocates of transitional bilingual education also believe that quality entails a long transition period, which is defined as the period during which a student is taught academics in his or her native or home language before being transferred to mainstream English-only classes. Colin Baker of the University of Wales, who has done an extensive review of studies that measure the effectiveness of bilingual education, calls such programs "stronger forms of bilingual education."

To advocates, quality bilingual education further requires well-trained, accredited bilingual teachers who effectively take charge of their classes. Finally, supporters of bilingual education maintain that effective native-language instruction requires parents' consent and participation, low teacher-student ratios, adequate school facilities, administrative support, and other enabling factors.

The National Association for Bilingual Education (NABE), a major advocacy organization, admits there are existing bilingual education programs that do not meet the above requirements. James J. Lyons, former NABE executive director, mentions a few of them:

> Some are bilingual in name only, staffed by monolingual English-speaking teachers with no professional preparation. . . . In a few instances, students have been assigned to bilingual education on the basis of an educationally irrelevant criterion such as surname. . . . In some localities, LEP [limited English proficient] students have been assigned to bilingual-education programs without the informed consent and choice of their parents.

Lyons argues that the existence of such malpractices does not warrant the elimination of a whole range of effective programs and the wholesale dismissal of the bilingual education policy.

## What the critics say

Critics of bilingual education maintain that the best way of teaching English to non-English speakers is not to instruct them in their home language but instead to immerse them in English. They often look to Canadian total French immersion, the approach adopted by Montreal, Canada, in teaching French to English-speaking, middle-class children. Under this program, native-English speakers start school entirely in French, with English introduced gradually. By the end of elementary school, most students become fluent in French, exhibit competence in English, and do well academically. The approach, which gained instant popularity, spread all throughout Canada and has become a model for other countries.

Critics of bilingual education in the United States find fault with the lengthy transition period during which Spanish speakers are immersed in their mother tongue before they move to the mainstream classes where they start learning English. They say that under established rules, the transition should only take three or four years, but that this rarely happens; in many cases, children stay with the mother tongue up to seven years, which, critics maintain, amounts to wasted time and lost opportunity.

Opponents also point out the lack of bilingual teachers nationwide, which renders existing bilingual programs questionable. Susan Headden, writing in *U.S. News & World Report*, comments, "Poorly trained teachers further complicate the picture. . . . The paucity of qualified candidates has forced desperate superintendents to waive some credentialing requirements and recruit instructors from abroad. The result is teachers who themselves struggle with English."

Most importantly, critics of bilingual education attribute much of the 30 percent high-school dropout rate among Hispanic children to their confinement to Spanish-only classrooms. They observe that the dropout rate is highest among ethnic groups, and that it has not decreased after many years of implementing bilingual instruction.

## California's Proposition 227

It was in reaction to these deficiencies that Proposition 227 was introduced in California in 1998. The initiative, which aimed to drastically restrict bilingual education in public schools and promote English-only instruction instead, was spearheaded by Ron C. Unz, a wealthy Silicon Valley entrepreneur. Unz believes that English is vital to scholastic achievement, economic success, the speedy integration of immigrants into society, and the preservation of national unity. Californians approved Proposition 227 with a 61 percent vote. According to a report by Kathleen Wilson and Jean Cowden Moore in the *Ventura County Star*, since the passage of Proposition 227 local school districts in California have reduced the number of students who are learning in Spanish to just 11 percent, down by almost two-thirds from 1997.

After his initiative was passed, Unz went on to spearhead a campaign called "English for the Children," which aims to make English the sole medium of instruction in public schools. Unz's campaign has won a few victories outside of California. Denver and Chicago have increased the amount of English instruction and limited TBE programs to three years. In 2000 Arizona, inspired by California's example and helped by Unz's resources, ended bilingual education. In 2002 Massachusetts approved a similar initiative against bilingual education. On the national level, various bills have been, albeit unsuccessfully, introduced in Congress either to end, reform, or restrict the federal role in bilingual education.

## Indefinite research leads to politicization

With restraints on bilingual education gaining momentum, the debate has become more intense. In the above-mentioned states that have legislated on the issue, both the pro-bilingual education camp and the pro-English camp have wooed politicians and advocacy organizations and raised large sums of money to support their cause.

Listening to the arguments of the two sides, it is easy to see that both have some valid points. However, research on the effectiveness of bilingual education, which should provide objective evidence to decide the issue, has not clearly determined which approaches work best. The relevant research over the past twenty years has been ambivalent: There is a substantial body of research that points to bilingual education's effectiveness, but there is also evidence indicating that English immersion is effective and that TBE programs may inhibit scholastic achievement. Professor of education Colin Baker attributes the contradictory research to the differing political agendas of those who favor and oppose bilingual education, which may influence the work of research institutions and individual researchers. Richard Rothstein, an analyst at the Economic Policy Institute in Washington, D.C., attributes the mixed results to the difficulty in measuring school achievement and isolating the individual factors that lead to it.

Without a final word on the subject, the debate between advocates and critics of bilingual education has become politicized. Many times, discussions have been conducted under the sponsorship of special-interest groups. Often, decisions have been made depending on who is in power in Washington, in the state capital, or the district. Bilingual education has been discussed alongside such volatile issues as nationalism, racism, immigration, and adoption of English as the official language of the United States as well as minority rights, cultural diversity, and the goals of education itself.

## Lobby groups and ethnic activists

Many supporters of bilingual education view the opposition to it as part of a nationwide movement to make English the official language of the United States and to restrict the use of ethnic languages. Advocates name two major organizations as the nemesis of bilingual education—U.S. English and English First—both of which advocate for the legislation of English as a national language and the adoption of government limits on the use of other languages.

U.S. English was founded by [U.S. former] Senator S.I. Hayakawa [of California] in 1983 to push for a constitutional amendment to make English the official language on both federal and state levels. However, critics of U.S. English view it as a racist lobby that aims to ban the use of ethnic languages. Pro-bilingual supporters note that two organizations funded by U.S. English—the Learning English Advocates Drive and Research in English Acquisition and Development—are at the forefront of campaigns seeking to reduce the scope of bilingual education in schools.

Commenting on the profile and history of U.S. English, journalist Andrew Phillips says the organization ran into controversy in the late 1980s after some leaders complained publicly that "Hispanics were breeding too fast." As a result, the organization was discredited and its officials were accused of racism. U.S. English claims it recovered in the late 1990s when its membership rose to 1 million and it had an annual budget of $15 million.

The second organization that supports English as an official national language is English First. Supporters of bilingual education often connect the organization to right-wing politicians, pointing out that it was once headed by Larry Pratt, founder and head of the lobby group Gun Owners of America, who later became adviser to former presidential contender Pat Buchanan.

## Countercharges from official-English groups

English-only proponents hurl back to the other camp similar charges, claiming that left-wing cultural activists are using the bilingual education debate to promote the Spanish language and Hispanic culture. Critics also argue that educators may wrongly support bilingual education in order to preserve the jobs of bilingual instructors. As John R. Silber, chancellor of Boston University, declares,

> Bilingual education is the interest of only two groups: one, bilingual educators, who face unemployment from the judgment of the people, and two, ethnic nationalists, for whom

the preservation and exaltation of immigrant language at the expense of English gives important political advantages to their English-speaking spokesmen. We must stop sacrificing the interests of our children to these two groups.

Ron C. Unz attributes the staying power of bilingual education to vested interests and what he calls the silence of the media. He says,

In this vast cavern of embarrassed media silence, the views of the overwhelmingly many were easily shouted down by the voices of the tiny but committed few. The story of the growth and entrenchment of these bilingual education programs constitutes a truly impressive and most remarkable illustration of the powerful dynamics of special-interest group politics.

In 1999 English-only proponents and the official-English movement gained a major victory when the House of Representatives finally passed a law mandating English as the country's official language. It was on this occasion that House Speaker Newt Gingrich declared, "Without English as a common language, there is no [American] civilization." The Senate, however, has not passed the legislation.

The claims and counterclaims, the accusations and rebuttals, are repeated again and again in various forums and media. In the absence of definitive research on whether bilingual education helps or harms students, the politicization of the bilingual education debate will certainly continue. With more state ballot initiatives on the issue expected to gain momentum in the coming years, the debate over bilingual education versus English-only classrooms will be hugging the headlines for the foreseeable future.

# 1

# Bilingual Education: A Historical Overview

## Colin Baker

*Colin Baker is a professor of education in the School of Education at the University of Wales at Bangor. He is the author of numerous books on bilingualism, including* Attitudes and Language, A Parents' and Teachers' Guide to Bilingualism, *the* Encyclopedia of Bilingualism and Bilingual Education *(with Sylvia Prys Jones), and* The Care and Education of Young Bilinguals.

The claim that bilingual education is a modern phenomenon is misplaced. In the United States, bilingual education flourished in the early immigrant settlements of the eighteenth and nineteenth centuries, up through the early twentieth century. Bilingualism suffered setbacks after the First World War as a result of anti-foreigner sentiments. It reemerged in the 1960s as a result of increased immigration and the rise of the civil rights movement, which espoused equality of educational opportunity. Through the years, the views of politicians, school administrators, and teachers on the subject have undergone significant changes in keeping with shifts in ideology and political realities.

One of the illusions about bilingual education is that it is a 20th century phenomenon. In the USA it may appear that bilingual education was born in the 1960s. The Canadian bilingual education movement is often charted from an experimental kindergarten class set up in St Lambert, Montreal, in 1965. In Ireland, bilingual education is sometimes presented as a child of the Irish Free State of 1922. The story of bilingual education in Wales often starts in 1939 with the establishment of the first Welsh-medium primary school. Despite these 20th century events, the historical origins of bilingual education lie well before this century.

The illusion of bilingual education as a modern phenomenon is dangerous on two counts. First, it fails to recognize that bilingual education has existed in one form or another for 5000 years or more. . . .

Second, there is a danger in isolating current bilingualism and bilingual education from their historical roots. In many countries (e.g. the USA, Canada, England and Sweden), bilingual education must be linked to the historical context of immigration as well as political movements such as civil rights, equality of educational opportunity, affirmative action and melting pot (integrationist, assimilationist) policies. Bilingual education in Ireland and Wales can only be properly analyzed by the rise of nationalism and language rights movements, for example. In Japan, language education policy has to be examined through movements from monolingual ideology to internationalism.

Bilingual education relates to debates about the fundamental purposes and aims of education in general: for individuals, communities, regions and nations. Bilingual education . . . is one component inside a wider social, economic, educational, cultural and political framework. As [Christina] Paulston observes: "unless we try in some way to account for the socio-historical, cultural, and economic-political factors which lead to certain forms of bilingual education, we will never understand the consequences of that education.". . .

## Linguistic diversity in the 18th and 19th centuries

In the United States, bilingual education has been determined partly by federal government and partly by state government, partly by local initiatives and partly by individuals (e.g. Proposition 227 in California). There has been neither total centralization nor devolution to states in bilingual education. Whilst states engage in much planning and policy-making, the federal government has exerted a powerful influence through funding, legislation and action in law. The federal government gives funds for education support services over and above state budgets.

Bilingual education in the United States has moved through considerable changes in the perspectives of politicians, administrators, educationalists and in school practice that indicate that shifts in ideology, preference and practice have occurred.

*The presence of different languages was frequently encouraged through religion, newspapers in different languages, and in both private and public schools.*

Long before European immigrants arrived in the United States, the land contained a variety of native (indigenous) languages. When the Italian, German, Dutch, French, Polish, Czech, Irish, Welsh and other immigrant groups arrived, there were already around 300 separate (Native American) languages in the United States. Immigrants brought with them a wide variety of languages. In the 18th and 19th centuries in the United States, up until the first World War, linguistic diversity was often accepted and the presence of different languages was frequently encouraged through religion, newspapers in different languages, and in both private and public schools.

There were exceptions to the acceptance of language diversity in this early period, such as Benjamin Franklin's anti-German stance in the

1750s, the Californian legislature mandating English-only instruction in 1855 and the ruthless language suppression policies of the Bureau of Indian Affairs in the 1880s. Thus, a high-profile and much-debated US language policy was not present until recent years; the concepts of "bilingualism" and "language minorities" were not part of a major national consciousness about language in the 18th and 19th centuries.

---

*[After World War I,] linguistic diversity was replaced by linguistic intolerance.*

---

However, there were early, pioneering examples of bilingual education in the United States as in the German-English schools. Set up by German communities in Ohio, Pennsylvania, Missouri, Minnesota, North and South Dakota and Wisconsin, bilingual as well as monolingual German education was accepted. Norwegian and Dutch were also languages of instruction within ethnic based schools. This openness to immigrant languages in the latter half of the 19th century was partly motivated by competition for students between public and private schools. Other factors such as benevolent (or uninterested) school administrators, the isolation of schools in rural areas, and ethnic homogeneity within an area also enabled a permissive attitude to mother tongue and bilingual education before World War I.

In most large cities in the latter half of the 19th century, English monolingual education was the dominant pattern. However, in cities such as Cincinnati, Baltimore, Denver and San Francisco, dual language education was present. In some schools in Cincinnati, for example, half the day was spent learning through German and the other half of the curriculum was delivered through English.

At the turn of the 20th century, Italian and Jewish immigrants were mostly placed in English-medium mainstream schools. However, examples of bilingual education existed and were permitted. For example, some Polish immigrants in Chicago attended Catholic schools where a small amount of teaching was through the mother tongue. So long as policy was within the jurisdiction of local towns and districts, the language of instruction did not become an issue in educational provision.

## Bilingual education in the 20th century

In the first two decades of the 20th century, a change in attitude to bilingualism and bilingual education occurred in the United States. A variety of factors are linked to this change and a subsequent restriction of bilingual education.

- The number of immigrants increased dramatically around the turn of the century. Classrooms in public schools were filled with immigrants. This gave rise to fears of new foreigners, and a call for the integration, harmonization and assimilation of immigrants. Immigrants' lack of English language and English literacy was a source of social, political and economic concern. The call for Americanization was sounded, with competence in English becoming associated with loyalty to the United States. The Nationality Act (1906) required immigrants to speak English to become naturalized Americans. The call for child literacy in English rather than child labor, socialization into a unified America rather than ethnic separation, along with increased centralized control, led to a belief in a common language for compulsory schooling.

- In 1919, the Americanization Department of the United States Bureau of Education adopted a resolution recommending "all states to prescribe that all schools, private and public, be conducted in the English language and that instruction in the elementary classes of all schools be in English". By 1923, 34 states had decreed that English must be the sole language of instruction in all elementary schools, public and private.

- A major influence on bilingual education in the United States came with the entry of the United States into the First World War in 1917. Anti-German feeling in the United States spread, with a consequent extra pressure for English monolingualism and a melting pot policy achieved through monolingual education. The German language was portrayed as a threat to the unity of Americanization. Linguistic diversity was replaced by linguistic intolerance. Schools became the tool for the assimilation and integration of diverse languages and cultures. Socialization into being American meant the elimination of languages and cultures other than English from schools. An interest in learning foreign languages declined.

This period was not totally restrictive. In 1923, the US Supreme Court declared that a Nebraska state law prohibiting the teaching of a foreign language to elementary school students was unconstitutional under the Fourteenth Amendment. This case, known as *Meyer v. Nebraska* concerned a case against a teacher for teaching a Bible story in German to a 10-year-old child. The original Nebraska ruling was that such mother-tongue teaching cultivated ideas and affections foreign to the best interests of the country. The Supreme Court, in overturning the Nebraska ruling, found that proficiency in a foreign language was "not injurious to the health, morals, or understanding of the ordinary child".

*[The Civil Rights] Act . . . symbolizes the beginning of a change in a less negative attitude to ethnic groups, and possibilities for increased tolerance of ethnic languages.*

This Supreme Court finding did not, in essence, support bilingualism or bilingual education. The Court observed that the desire of a state legislature to foster a homogeneous people was "easy to appreciate.". . .

In 1957, the Russians launched their Sputnik into space. For United States politicians and public, a period of soul-searching led to debates about the quality of US education, US scientific creativity and US competence to compete in an increasingly international world. Doubts arose about the hitherto over-riding concern with English as the melting-pot language, and a new consciousness was aroused about the need for foreign language instruction. In 1958, the National Defense and Education Act was passed, promoting foreign language learning in elementary schools, high-schools and universities. This, in turn, helped to create a slightly more soul-searching attitude to languages other than English spoken among ethnic groups in the USA.

## The Civil Rights movement

In the United States in the 1960s, various other factors allowed a few opportunities to bring back bilingual education, albeit in a disparate, semi-isolated manner. The "opportunity" movement for bilingual schools to be re-established in the United States needs to be understood in the wider perspective of the Civil Rights movement, the struggle for the rights of African-Americans, and the call to establish general equality of opportunity (and equality of educational opportunity) for all people, irrespective of race, color or creed. The 1964 Civil Rights Act prohibited discrimination on the basis of color, race or national origin, and led to the establishment of the Office of Civil Rights. This Act is an important marker that symbolizes the beginning of a change in a less negative attitude to ethnic groups, and possibilities for increased tolerance of ethnic languages, at least at the Federal level.

*There have been moves against an emergence of a strong version of bilingual education, particularly [among groups] that seek to establish English monolingualism and cultural assimilation.*

The restoration of the practice of bilingual education in the USA is often regarded as starting in 1963, in one school in Florida. In 1963, Cuban exiles established a dual language school (Coral Way Elementary School) in Dade County in South Florida. Believing they were only in exile for a short period, the educated, middle-class Cubans set up this Spanish-English bilingual school. The need to maintain their mother tongue of Spanish was aided by (1) highly trained professional teachers being ready to work in such schools, (2) the Cubans' plight as victims of a harsh Communist state, and (3) their expected temporary stay in the United States. Their unquestioned loyalty to United States' policies and democratic politics gained sympathy for the Cubans. Bilingual education in Dade County received both political support and funding. . . .

While the re-establishment of bilingual schools in the USA has benefited from the example and success of Coral Way Elementary School an understanding of bilingual education in the United States requires a grasp of legislation and lawsuits.

In 1967, a Texas Senator, Ralph Yarborough, introduced a Bilingual Education Act as an amendment of the 1965 Elementary and Secondary Education Act. The legislation was designed to help mother tongue Spanish speakers who were seen as failing in the school system. Enacted in 1968 as Title VII of the Elementary and Secondary Education Act, the Bilingual Education Act indicated that bilingual education programs were to be seen as part of federal educational policy. It authorized the use of federal funds for the education of speakers of languages other than English. It also undermined the English-only legislation still lawful in many states. The 1968 Bilingual Education Act also allocated funds for such minority language speakers while they shifted to working through English in the classroom.

## Lau remedies

A landmark in United States' bilingual education was a lawsuit. A court case was brought on behalf of Chinese students against the San Francisco School District in 1970. The case concerned whether or not non-English speaking students received equal educational opportunities when instructed in a language they could not understand. The failure to provide bilingual education was alleged to violate both the equal protection clause of the 14th Amendment and Title VI of the Civil Rights Act of 1964. The case, known as *Lau versus Nichols*, was rejected by the federal district court and a court of appeals, but was accepted by the Supreme Court in 1974. The verdict outlawed English submersion programs for language minority children and resulted in nationwide "Lau remedies". The Supreme Court ruled that "There is no equality of treatment merely by providing students with the same facilities, textbooks, teachers and curriculum; for students who do not understand English are effectively foreclosed from any meaningful education."

The Lau remedies acknowledged that students not proficient in English needed help. Such remedies included English as a Second Language classes, English tutoring and some form of bilingual education. The Lau remedies created some expansion in the use of minority languages in schools although the accent nationally was still on a transitional use of the home language for English language learners.

The Lau court case is symbolic of the dynamic and continuing contest to establish language rights in the USA particularly through testing the law in the courtroom. However, the kind of bilingual education needed to achieve equality of educational opportunity for language minority children was not defined although the right to equal opportunity for language minorities was asserted. The means of achieving that right was not declared. Nevertheless, during this era, there was a modest growth in developmental maintenance bilingual education and ethnic community mother tongue schools. . . .

Since the 1980s, there have been moves against an emergence of a strong version of bilingual education, particularly found in the rise of pressure groups such as English First and US English that seek to establish English monolingualism and cultural assimilation. . . . In recent decades in the USA, bilingual education has become contentious, as will now be illustrated.

To understand the current period, it is helpful to examine the legislative changes with respect to bilingual education in the United States. We return to the 1968 Bilingual Education Act (Title VII and part of the Elementary and Secondary Education Act). This provided a compensatory "poverty program" for the educationally disadvantaged among language minorities. It did not require schools to use a child's home language other than English. However, it did allow a few educators to bring "home languages" into the classroom rather than exclude them. The 1974 amendments to this Bilingual Education Act required schools receiving grants to include teaching in a student's home language and culture so as to allow the child to progress effectively through the educational system. Effective progress in student achievement could occur via the home language or via English. However, this gave rise to fierce debates about how much a student's native language should be used in school. . . . Some argued that it was essential to develop a child's speaking and literacy skills in their native language before English was introduced in a major way. Others argued that educational equality of opportunity could best be realized by teaching English as early as possible and assimilating language minority children into mainstream culture.

In 1978, the United States Congress reauthorized Transitional Bilingual Education, allowing the native language to be used only to the extent necessary for a child to achieve competence in the English language. Title VII funds could not be used for Maintenance Bilingual Education programs. The 1984 and 1988 amendments allowed increasing percentages of the funds available to be allocated to programs where a students' first language was not used.

## Hostility to bilingual education

The Reagan administration was generally hostile to bilingual education. In the *New York Times* on the 3rd March 1981, President Reagan is quoted as saying that "It is absolutely wrong and against the American concept to have a bilingual education program that is now openly, admittedly, dedicated to preserving their native language and never getting them adequate in English so they can go out into the job market". Reagan believed that preservation of the native language meant neglect of English language acquisition. Bilingual education programs were seen as serving to neglect English language competence in students. Reagan dismissed bilingual education in favor of submersion and transitional programs.

In 1985, William Bennett, the then Secretary of Education, suggested that there was no evidence that children from language minorities (whom the Bilingual Education Act had sought to help), had benefited from this Act. Some 25% of funds were made available for English monolingual, alternative instructional programs (e.g. Structured English programs; Sheltered English programs). This represented a further political dismissal of education through the minority language and a dismissal of "strong" forms of bilingual education.

The Lau remedies were withdrawn by the Reagan government and do not have the force of law. The federal government left local politicians to create their own policies. [Rights to bilingual education in the United States underwent further changes through the years.] Legislation and litigation has often led to "weak" forms of bilingual education (e.g. transitional bilingual education). Also, recent legislation has not tended to increase rights to a bilingual education. During the Reagan and Bush Presidencies in the United States, the accent was more on submersion and transitional bilingual education. The right to early education through a minority language failed to blossom in those years.

In 1994, the 103rd Congress undertook a major reform of education through legislation entitled Goals 2000; Educate America Act, and also by the Improving America's Schools Act. This extensive reform included an acknowledgement that students for whom English was a second language ("Limited English Proficient" students) should be expected to achieve high academic standards. Such legislation aimed to provide children with an enriched educational program, improving instructional strategies and making the curriculum more challenging. The improving America's Schools Act of 1994 reauthorized Title VII, strengthening the state role by requiring state educational authorities to review Title VII appropriations and provide additional funds for specific groups such as immigrants. Thus the reauthorization of Title VII in 1994 continued federal support for bilingual education programs.

## Moving toward a broader perspective

Since Title VII of the Improving America's Schools Act of 1994, halting attempts have been made to move away from remedial, compensatory and deficiency models of bilingual education to more innovative models. For example, priority has been given to funding school reform where there is the clear aim to raise standards across the curriculum for all children. In doing this, bilingual children have the opportunity to reach high levels of skills to help develop the nation's human resources and improve US competitiveness in a global market. Thus school districts have been encouraged to create comprehensive school reform plans where bilingual instruction or English as a second language are incorporated into an overall holistic "raising standards" school system. From 1994, the issue about bilingual education moved from being narrowly focused on the language of instruction to a broader range of questions being asked about the quality and standards of education being given to language minority students.

Opponents of bilingual education in the United States do not generally oppose foreign language programs for English speakers. Such programs are regarded as important in educating students for the global economy. Some forms of bilingualism (e.g. English-Japanese, English-German) are seen to be of value for US economic prosperity. One of the goals of the National Education Goals Panel of 1994 was thus that the percentage of students who are competent in more than one language should substantially increase. The 1994 Amendments to the Bilingual Education Act meant that proficient bilingualism became a desirable goal when it brought economic benefits to individuals and particularly to the nation. Hence the Amendments resulted in funding for a larger number of dual language programs.

However, the reauthorization of Title VII came under attack both by politicians and the US Press. Congress considered legislation to repeal the law and eliminate its funding. Whilst this did not succeed, it nevertheless pointed to a dominant political and mass media—being against bilingual education. Title VII appropriations were reduced by 38% between 1994 and 1996 leading to cuts in bilingual programs, in teacher training and reducing the budgets for research, evaluation and support of bilingual education in the United States.

[As of 1998] the estimated number of school-age speakers of languages in addition to English is around 6,670,000 or 13% of the school population. The number of "Limited English Proficient" (LEP) students is around three and a half million forming approximately 22% of students in California, 13% in Texas, 12% in Florida, 11.5% in Arizona and 7.5% in New York. Some three-quarters of such "LEP" students were reported as being enrolled in programs to meet their English language needs. However, around 88% of such "LEP" students are in Title I (Compensatory Education Programs), Emergency Immigrant Education, Migrant or Special Education programs. Only 0.4% are in transitional bilingual education programs and 0.1% are in developmental bilingual education. . . .

Two conclusions. First, there is common perception that educational policy is often static, always conservative and very slow to change. The history of bilingual education in the United States tends to falsify and contradict such beliefs. Such history shows that there is constant change, a constant movement in ideas, ideology and impetus. There is action and reaction, movement and contra-movement, assertion and response. One conclusion is that change will always occur in bilingual education policy and provision. Nothing is static. While there will be periods when bilingual education is criticized, forbidden and rejected, there will be reactions, with the possibility of more positive, accepting periods ahead. There is no certainty in the future history of bilingual education, only uncertainty and change. Yet uncertainty and change provide occasional opportunities for bilingual education to progress.

Second, the conclusion must not be that bilingual education moves from more positive "golden' times" to being dismissed and rejected. The history of bilingual education in the Basque Country and Wales follows a different sequence. In these countries, bilingual education has moved from being dismissed and suppressed to considerable expansion. From a time when Welsh was banned in the classroom, there is currently a widespread acceptance and provision of bilingual education in Wales. No universal patterns of change can or should be deduced from either the United States or the Welsh experience. Such unpredictability provides a challenge to bilingual educators.

# 2

# Bilingual Education Has Led to the Segregation of Non-English-Speaking Students

Rosalie Pedalino Porter

*Rosalie Pedalino Porter is the director of the Institute for Research in English Acquisition and Development (READ) in Amherst, Massachusetts, and editor of the organization's publication,* Perspectives. *She is the author of the book* Forked Tongue: the Politics of Bilingual Education, *which refutes the assumptions and claims of bilingual education.*

Since the official adoption of bilingual education in 1968, bilingual education, in most instances, has meant teaching language minority students their native languages before they are taught English. As a result, these students are taught in their native language (most often Spanish) for as long as six years, delaying their acquisition of English. This process has segregated non-English-speaking students from English-speaking students, with gaps in learning and achievement between them. The goals of bilingual education are English language mastery and academic achievement in English, but when a student's acquisition of English is delayed, these goals are jeopardized.

Bilingual education is a classic example of an experiment that was begun with the best of humanitarian intentions but has turned out to be terribly wrong-headed. To understand this experiment, we need to look back to the mid-1960s, when the civil-rights movement for African-Americans was at its height and Latino activists began to protest the damaging circumstances that led to unacceptably high proportions of school dropouts among Spanish-speaking children—more than 50 percent nationwide. Latino leaders borrowed the strategies of the civil-rights movement, calling for legislation to address the needs of Spanish-speaking children—Cubans in Florida, Mexicans along the southern border, Puerto Ricans in the Northeast. In 1968 Congress approved a bill filed by Senator Ralph Yarborough, of Texas, aimed at removing the language barrier to an equal education. The Bilingual Education Act was a modestly funded ($7.5 million for the first year) amendment to the Elementary and Secondary Education Act of 1965, intended to help poor Mexican-American children learn English. At the time, the goal was "not to keep any specific language alive," Yarborough said. "It is not the purpose of the bill to create pockets of different languages through the country . . . but just to try to make those children fully literate in English."

English was not always the language of instruction in American schools. During the eighteenth century classes were conducted in German, Dutch, French, and Swedish in some schools in Pennsylvania, Maryland, and Virginia. From the mid nineteenth to the early twentieth century, classes were taught in German in several cities across the Midwest. For many years French was taught and spoken in Louisiana schools, Greek in Pittsburgh. Only after the First World War, when German was proscribed, did public sentiment swing against teaching in any language but English.

---

*The goals of bilingual education [are] English-language mastery and academic achievement in English in mainstream classrooms.*

---

These earlier decisions on education policy were made in school, church, city, or state. Local conditions determined local school policy. But in 1968, for the first time, the federal government essentially dictated how non-English-speaking children should be educated. That action spawned state laws and legal decisions in venues all the way up to the Supreme Court. No end of money and effort was poured into a program that has since become the most controversial arena in public education.

## From transition to segregation

In simplest terms, bilingual education is a special effort to help immigrant children learn English so that they can do regular schoolwork with their English-speaking classmates and receive an equal educational opportunity. But what it is in the letter and the spirit of the law is not what it has become in practice. Some experts decided early on that children should be taught for a time in their native languages, so that they would continue to learn other subjects while learning English. It was expected that the transition would take a child three years.

From this untried experimental idea grew an education industry that expanded far beyond its original mission to teach English and resulted in the extended segregation of non-English-speaking students. In practice, many bilingual programs became more concerned with teaching in the native language and maintaining the ethnic culture of the family than with teaching children English in three years.

Beginning in the 1970s several notions were put forward to provide a rationale, after the fact, for the bilingual-teaching experiment. Jose Cardenas, the director emeritus of the Intercultural Development Research Association, in San Antonio, and Blandina Cardenas (no relation), an associate professor of educational administration at the University of Texas at San Antonio, published their "theory of incompatibilities." According to this theory, Mexican-American children in the United States are so different from "majority" children that they must be given bilingual and bicultural instruction in order to achieve academic success. Educators were convinced of the soundness of the idea—an urgent need for special teaching for non-English-speaking children—and judges handed down court decisions on the basis of it.

Jim Cummins, a bilingual-education theorist and a professor of education at the University of Toronto, contributed two hypotheses. His "developmental interdependence" hypothesis suggests that learning to read in one's native language facilitates reading in a second language. His "threshold" hypothesis suggests that children's achievement in the second language depends on the level of their mastery of their native language and that the most-positive cognitive effects occur when both languages are highly developed. Cummins's hypotheses were interpreted to mean that a solid foundation in native-language literacy and subject-matter learning would best prepare students for learning in English. In practice these notions work against the goals of bilingual education—English-language mastery and academic achievement in English in mainstream classrooms.

## The benefits of bilingual education

Bilingual education has heightened awareness of the needs of immigrant, migrant, and refugee children. The public accepts that these children are entitled to special help; we know that the economic well-being of our society depends on maintaining a literate population with the academic competence for higher education and skilled jobs. The typical complaint heard years ago, "My grandfather came from Greece [or Sicily or Poland] and they didn't do anything special for him, and he did okay," no longer figures in the public discussion.

Bilingual education has brought in extra funding to hire and train paraprofessionals, often the parents of bilingual children, as classroom aides. Career programs in several school districts, among them an excellent one in Seattle that was in operation through early 1996, pay college tuition for paraprofessionals so that they may qualify as teachers, thus attracting more teachers from immigrant communities to the schools. Large school districts such as those in New York and Los Angeles have long had bilingual professionals on their staffs of psychologists, speech therapists, social workers, and other specialists.

*Surveys of the parents of limited-English schoolchildren have shown that a large majority consider learning English . . . to be of much greater importance than receiving instruction in the native language.*

Promoting parental understanding of American schools and encouraging parental involvement in school activities are also by-products of bilingual education. Workshops and training sessions for all educators on the historical and cultural backgrounds of the rapidly growing and varied ethnic communities in their districts result in greater understanding of and respect for non-English-speaking children and their families. These days teachers and school administrators make an effort to communicate with parents who have a limited command of English, by sending letters and school information to them at home in their native languages and by employing interpreters when necessary for parent-teacher conferences. In all these ways bilingual education has done some good.

## A lack of evidence

But has it produced the desired results in the classroom? The accumulated research of the past thirty years reveals almost no justification for teaching children in their native languages to help them learn either English or other subjects—and these are the chief objectives of all legislation and judicial decisions in this field. Self-esteem is not higher among limited-English students who are taught in their native languages, and stress is not higher among children who are introduced to English from the first day of school—though self-esteem and stress are the factors most often cited by advocates of bilingual teaching.

The final report of the Hispanic Dropout Project (issued in February 1998) states,

> While the dropout rate for other school-aged populations has declined, more or less steadily, over the last 25 years, the overall Hispanic dropout rate started higher and has remained between 30 and 35 percent during that same time period . . . 2.5 times the rate for blacks and 3.5 times the rate for white non-Hispanics.

About one out of every five Latino children never enters a U.S. school, which inflates the Latino dropout rate. According to a 1995 report on the dropout situation from the National Center on Education Statistics, speaking Spanish at home does not correlate strongly with dropping out of high school; what does correlate is having failed to acquire English-language ability. The NCES report states,

> For those youths that spoke Spanish at home, English speaking ability was related to their success in school. . . . The status dropout rate for young Hispanics reported to speak English 'well' or 'very well' was . . . 19.2 percent, a rate similar to the 17.5 percent status dropout rate observed for enrolled Hispanic youths that spoke only English at home.

In the past ten years several national surveys of the parents of limited-English schoolchildren have shown that a large majority consider learning English and having other subjects taught in English to be of much greater importance than receiving instruction in the native language or about the native culture. In 1988 the Educational Testing Service conducted a national Parent Preference Study among 2,900 Cuban, Mexican, Puerto Rican, and Asian parents with children in U.S. public schools. Although most of the parents said they wanted special help for their children in learning English and other subjects, they differed on whether their children should be taught in their native languages. Asian parents were the most heavily opposed to the use of native languages in the schools. Among Latino groups, the Puerto Rican parents were most in favor, the Mexicans somewhat less, and the Cubans least of all. A large majority of the parents felt that it is the family's duty, not the school's, to teach children about the history and traditions of their ancestors. When Mexican parents were asked if they wanted the school to teach reading and writing in Spanish and English, 70 percent answered yes. But when they were asked if they wanted Spanish taught in school if it meant less time for teaching English, only 12 percent were in favor.

## Public support for English

In the most recent national survey of Latino parents, published by the Center for Equal Opportunity, in Washington, D.C., 600 Latino parents of school-age children were interviewed (in Spanish or English) in five U.S. cities—Houston, Los Angeles, Miami, New York, and San Antonio. A strong majority favored learning English as the first order of business for their children, considering it more important than learning other subjects, and much more important than reading and writing in Spanish.

Having begun quietly in the 1980s and gained momentum in the 1990s, Latino opposition to native-language teaching programs is now publicly apparent. Two actions by communities of Latino parents demonstrate this turn of events.

A hundred and fifty parents with children in Brooklyn public schools filed a lawsuit in September of 1995, charging that because their children routinely remained segregated in bilingual programs in excess of three years, and in some cases in excess of six years, contrary to section 3204 (2) of the State Education Law, these children were not receiving adequate instruction in English, "the crucial skill that leads to equal opportunity in schooling, jobs, and public life in the United States."

New York State law limits participation in a bilingual program to three years, but an extension can be granted for up to three years more if an individual review of the student's progress seems to warrant it. And here is the nub of the lawsuit: thousands of students are routinely kept in native-language classrooms for six years or longer without even the pretense of individual progress reviews.

Unfortunately, even with the help of a strong champion of their cause, Sister Kathy Maire, and the pro bono services of a prestigious New York law firm, Paul, Weiss, Rifkind, Wharton & Garrison, the parents lost their case. Under New York law these parents in fact have the right not to enroll their children in bilingual classes, or to remove them from bilingual classes, but in practice pressure from school personnel is almost impossible to overcome. Teachers and principals tell parents that their children will fail in English-language classrooms. They play on ethnic pride, asserting that children of a Latino background need to be taught in Spanish to improve their self-esteem.

In May of [1997] the Court of Appeals of the State of New York ruled that there could be no further appeals. But the publicity attracted by the case may encourage other Latino parents to take action on behalf of their children. And one concrete improvement has already occurred: the New York City Board of Education announced an end in 1996 to the automatic testing for English-language skills that children with Spanish surnames had undergone when they started school.

## Protests in Los Angeles

On the other coast an equally irate group of Latino parents moved against the Ninth Street School in Los Angeles. Seventy families of mostly Mexican garment workers planned the protest through Las Familias del Pueblo, a community organization that provides after-school child care. Typical of the protesters are Selena and Carlos (I have changed their names, because they are undocumented immigrants), who left the poverty of a rural Mexican village in 1985 to come to work in Los Angeles. Their children were born in Los Angeles, but the school insisted that they not be taught in English until they had learned to read and write in Spanish, by the fourth or fifth grade. The parents complained to the school for years that children who lived in Spanish-speaking homes and neighborhoods needed to study in English in the primary grades, when children find it easier to learn a language than they will later on.

Persistent stonewalling by administrators finally moved the parents to keep their children out of school for nearly two weeks in February of 1996, a boycott that made national news. The parents demanded that their children be placed in English-language classes, a demand that has since been met. The school administrators waited too long to make this change: the previous spring only six students (about one percent of enrollment) had been deemed sufficiently fluent in English to "graduate" to regular classrooms in the next school year.

In the early 1970s almost all the students in bilingual classes spoke Spanish. Today, of the three million limited-English students in U.S. public schools, more than 70 percent speak Spanish at home; the rest speak any of 327 other languages. California alone enrolls 1.4 million limited-English children in its schools—one of every four students in the state. According to the 1990 U.S. census, 70 percent of limited-English students are concentrated in California, Florida, Illinois, New Jersey, New York, and Texas.

---

*Controversy over native-language education is at the boil in California.*

---

Controversy over native-language education is at the boil in California. In our most multicultural state, where minorities now constitute 46 percent of the population, a revolution is brewing. In 1987 the California legislature failed to reauthorize the Bilingual-Bicultural Education Act, allowing it to expire. However, the California Department of Education immediately notified all school districts that even without the state law the same requirements would be enforced and bilingual programs continued. In July of 1995 the state Board of Education announced two major policy changes: the "preference" for native-language programs would henceforth be revoked and school districts would be given as much flexibility as possible in choosing their own programs; and school districts were ordered to be more diligent in recording evidence of student achievement than in describing the teaching methods used.

Yet in two years only four school districts have succeeded in obtaining waivers from the department, permitting them to initiate English-language programs for limited-English students. Why should schools have to seek waivers when no state or federal law, no court decision, no state policy, bars them from teaching in English? The most important case to date is that of the Orange Unified School District, with 7,000 limited-English students.

Orange Unified applied in early May of [1997] for permission to focus on English-language teaching in kindergarten through sixth grade while using a small amount of Spanish. The Department of Education strongly opposed the district, as did the California Association for Bilingual Education, California Rural Legal Assistance, and the organization Multicultural Education, Training, and Advocacy (META). Local Latino activists publicly criticized the district's change of plan, and some bilingual teachers resigned.

Nevertheless, the Board of Education last July [1997] granted Orange permission to try an English-language program for one year. A lawsuit was filed, and a temporary restraining order granted. But [in] September, U.S. District Court Judge William B. Shubb lifted the restraining order. In his seventeen-page decision the judge wrote, "The court will not second-guess the educational policy choices made by educational authorities." And he added a ruling with much broader application:

> It is clear that "appropriate action" does not require "bilingual education.". . . The alleged difference between two sound LEP [Limited-English Proficient] educational theories—ESL [English as a Second Language] and bilingual instruction—is inadequate to demonstrate irreparable harm.

The federal court ruling allowed Orange to proceed with its English-language program. But the case was returned to Sacramento County Superior Court, where Judge Ronald B. Robie ruled that nothing in California state law requires primary-language instruction, and therefore no waiver is needed for a district to provide an English-language program; and that federal law permits educational programs not to include native-language instruction. Soon after Robie's ruling the Board of Education rescinded the policy that schools must obtain waivers in order to eliminate bilingual programs. Although the court decision may be appealed, these two actions signal a victory for Orange Unified and have implications for other California districts as well. The legal battle has already cost the Orange district $300,000, which no doubt would have been better spent on students. It is estimated that the new program will cost an additional $60,000 the first year, but the superintendent of Orange Unified schools, Robert French, says, "We're not doing this to save money. We're doing this to save kids."

Ron Unz, a Silicon Valley entrepreneur, has long been concerned about the California education system's failures, especially as they affect its 1.4 million limited-English students. He has decided to put his time, energy, and money into an initiative—"English for the Children"—meant to give all California voters a say on the language of public education. If the initiative passes, in elections to be held on June 2, it will give "preference" to English-language programs for immigrant children, reduce the length of time children may remain in special programs, and make the state spend $50 million a year to teach English to adults. Bilingual programs will be allowed only in localities where parents actually request native-language teaching for their children. [Editor's note: California voters approved the "English for Children" initiative—also known as Proposition 227—in June 1998.]

# 3

# Bilingual Education Has Not Inhibited Immigrant Assimilation

## Richard Rothstein

*Richard Rothstein is a research associate of the Economic Policy Institute at Washington, D.C. This viewpoint is adapted from his book* The Way We Were?: The Myths and Realities of America's Student Achievement.

Through the years, research findings on the effectiveness or non-effectiveness of bilingual education and English-only approaches have not been definitive. This has allowed the intense debate between proponents and opponents of bilingual education to continue. Both sides cite case studies to support their claims, but they may never achieve satisfaction as studies cannot really control the complex factors that affect student achievement. Some students have clearly benefited from English-only programs, while others have benefited from bilingual education. The one conclusion that can be drawn from the available data is that there is no obvious crisis surrounding bilingual education, as new immigrant groups have steadily moved up the socioeconomic ladder over the last several decades.

When bilingual education began to reemerge in the 1970s—spurred by a Supreme Court finding that schools without special provisions for educating language-minority children were not providing equal education—the nation's memory of [the historical] precedents [of bilingual education] had been erased. Today many Americans blithely repeat the myth that, until the recent emergence of separatist minority activists and their liberal supporters, the nation had always immersed its immigrant children in nothing but English and this method had proved its effectiveness.

This mixed history, however, does not prove that bilingual education is effective, any more so than English immersion or intense English-language instruction. To an unbiased layperson, the arguments of both advocates and opponents of bilingual education seem to make sense. On the one hand, it's reasonable to insist that children who don't speak English continue their education in a language they understand in history, literature, math, and science, while they learn English. It's also reasonable to expect, however, that this might make it too tempting to defer English-language instruction. Moreover, the best way to do something difficult—e.g., making the transition to English—is simply to do it without delay. It makes sense to acknowledge that children may adapt better to school if the school's culture is not in conflict with that of the home. But some immigrant parents may be more intent on preserving native culture for their children than are the children themselves.

---

*As with all educational research, it is so difficult to control for complex background factors that affect academic outcomes that no single study is ultimately satisfying.*

---

Modern research findings on bilingual education are mixed. As with all educational research, it is so difficult to control for complex background factors that affect academic outcomes that no single study is ultimately satisfying. Bilingual education advocates point to case studies of primary-language programs in Calexico, California; Rock Point, Arizona; Santa Fe, New Mexico; New Haven, Connecticut; and elsewhere that show that children advance further in both English and other academic subjects when native-language instruction is used and the transition to English is very gradual. Opponents point to case studies in Redwood City and Berkeley, California; in Fairfax, Virginia; and elsewhere that prove that immersion in English or rapid and intensive English instruction is most effective. Overall, the conflicting evidence from these case studies does not suggest that abolition of bilingual education or even the substitution of parental choice for pedagogical expertise in determining whether bilingual approaches should be used would improve things much.

The problem is especially complex because not only economic factors but also generational variation apparently affects the achievement of immigrant youths. In 1936, the principal of a high school in New York City that enrolled large numbers of Italian immigrants wrote:

> The problem of juvenile delinquency . . . baffles all the forces of organized society. . . . The highest rate of delinquency is characteristic of immigrant communities. . . . The delinquent is usually the American-born child of foreign-born parents, not the immigrant himself. Delinquency, then, is fundamentally a second-generation problem. This intensifies the responsibility of the school.

The same is true today. The challenge now facing immigrant educators is that academic achievement for second-generation Hispanic and Asian children is often below that of children who arrive in the U.S. as immigrants themselves. Many of these children of the second generation seem to speak English, but they are fully fluent in neither English nor their home language. Many of their parents, frustrated that their own ambition has not been transmitted to their children, may become convinced that only English immersion will set their children straight, while others seek bilingual solutions to prevent the corruption of American culture from dampening their children's ambition.

## Politicizing the issue

In the absence of persuasive evidence, the issue has become politicized. In a country as large as ours, with as varied experience, there is virtually no limit to the anecdotes and symbols that can be invoked as substitutes for evidence.

Opponents of bilingual education promote Hispanic parents to the media when they claim they want their children to learn English without bilingual support; the clear implication is that only liberal ideologues and separatists support native-language instruction. These claims . . . may not reflect the feelings of most parents. And the technology of teaching a new language to immigrant children is complex; both bilingual education advocates and opponents claim their goal is full English literacy as rapidly as possible. But there's no reason to expect that politicized parent groups are the best judges of language acquisition research.

There are also successful adult immigrants who brag of their English fluency, acquired either with or without bilingual education. As always, such anecdotal evidence should be treated with caution. Richard Rodriguez' autobiography, *Hunger of Memory*, describes his successful education in an English-only environment. But Rodriguez, unlike most immigrants, was raised in a predominantly English-speaking neighborhood and was the only Spanish speaker in his class. His experience may be relevant for some immigrants, but not relevant for many others.

> *Bilingual instruction has never interfered with the powerful assimilationist influences that overwhelm all children whose parents migrate here.*

Whichever method is, in fact, more effective for most immigrant children, there will be many for whom the other method worked well. It may be the case that immigrant children's social and economic background characteristics should affect the pedagogy chosen. Even if some Russian Jewish immigrants did not require bilingual education to graduate from high school, perhaps Italians would have progressed more rapidly if they'd had access to bilingual instruction. Today, the fact that some (though not all) Asian immigrants seem to progress rapidly in school without native-language support provides no relevant evidence about whether this model can work well for Mexican or Caribbean children, especially those low on the ladder of socioeconomic status and those whose parents have little education. Nor does it tell us much about what the best pedagogy would be for Asians who generally do less well in school, such as Hmong, Laotian, and Cambodian children.

It is certain, however, that the American "melting pot" has never been endangered by pluralist efforts to preserve native languages and cultures. Bilingual instruction has never interfered with the powerful assimilationist influences that overwhelm all children whose parents migrate here. And this is equally true of Spanish-speaking children today.

After the last 20 years of bilingual education throughout America, Spanish-speaking children continue to assimilate. From 1972 to 1995, despite rapidly accelerating immigration (more Hispanic youths are first-generation immigrants today than 20 years ago), the Hispanic high school completion rate has crept upward (from 66% to 70%). Hispanic high school graduates who enroll in college jumped from 45% to 54% (for non-Hispanic whites, it's now 64%). And the number of Hispanic high school graduates who subsequently complete four years of college jumped from 11% to 16% (for non-Hispanic whites, it's now 34%). A study of the five-county area surrounding Los Angeles, the most immigrant-affected community in the nation, found that from 1980 to 1990, the share of U.S.-born Hispanics in professional occupations grew from 7% to 9%, the share in executive positions grew from 7% to 10%, and the share in other administrative and technical jobs grew from 24% to 26%. Overall, 55% of U.S.-born Hispanics are in occupations for which a good education is a necessity, in an area where bilingual education has been practiced for the last generation.

Perhaps we can do better. Perhaps we would do better with less bilingual education. But perhaps not. All we can say for sure is that the data reveal no apparent crisis, and the system for immigrant education with which we've been muddling through, with all its problems, does not seem to be in a state of collapse.

The best thing that could happen to the bilingual education debate would be to remove it from the political realm. Sound-bite pedagogy is no cure for the complex interaction of social, economic, and instructional factors that determine the outcomes of contemporary American schools.

# 4

# Bilingual Education Harms Non-English-Speaking Students

## Peter Duignan

*Peter Duignan, a senior fellow emeritus at the Hoover Institution, has written and edited more than forty books and monographs, including* The Hispanics in the United States: A History *(with L.H. Gann) and* The Rebirth of the West: The Americanization of the Democratic World, 1945–1958.

Most studies done by independent researchers show that bilingual education does not work, is costly, is divisive, and inhibits Spanish speakers' ability to compete in American society. Hispanics taught in bilingual programs tend to fall behind their peers, drop out of school at a high rate, and end up in low-paying jobs. However, bilingual education continues to survive in schools because of the insistence of some members of the education bureaucracy and the efforts of cultural activists who promote the teaching of the Spanish language and culture for ideological reasons.

Some members of the education bureaucracy, guided by the principle of "cultural maintenance," want Hispanic-surnamed children to continue to be taught Spanish language and culture and English only as a second language. The extremists among them even want Spanish to be a second national language. The Center for Equal Opportunity's president and CEO, Linda Chavez, accuses these advocates of bilingual education of being politicized and manipulated by cultural activists. The programs they favor, she claims, have failed and have undermined the future of the Latino children they were meant to help. Chavez's criticisms are supported by the evidence. Latinos, Hispanics, or Chicanos taught in bilingual programs test behind peers taught in English-only classrooms, drop out of school at a high rate, and are trapped in low-skilled, low-paying jobs.

. . . the problem began in 1974 when the Supreme Court in *Lau v. Nichols* ignored two hundred years of English-only instruction in Ameri-

31

ca's schools and said that students who did not speak English must receive special treatment from local schools. This allowed an enormous expansion of bilingual education. Advocates of bilingual education in the U.S. Office for Civil Rights had begun a small program in 1968 to educate Mexican American children, but by 1996 it had expanded from a $7.5 million to an $8 billion a year industry. The initial objective to teach English to Spanish speakers for one or two years was perverted into a program to Hispanicize, not Americanize, Spanish speakers. The federal program insists that 75 percent of education tax dollars be spent on bilingual education, that is, long-term native-language programs, not English as a second language. Asians, Africans, and Europeans are all in mainstream classes and receive extra training in English-as-a-second-language programs for a few hours a day. Hispanic students, in contrast, are taught in Spanish 70 to 80 percent of the time. New York is especially irresponsible in this regard, forcing children with Spanish surnames, even those who speak no Spanish at home, to take Spanish and to spend at least 40 percent of the class time in Spanish classes. New England schools are about as bad, forcing Spanish- and Portuguese-surnamed children to take Spanish or Crioulo!

## Bilingual education creates an underclass

Some critics of bilingualism claim that the vast majority of Spanish speakers want their children to be taught in English, not Spanish, and do not want the U.S. government to keep up Hispanic culture and language. The bilingual bureaucracy at local and federal levels wants to Hispanicize and to capture federal funds for schools. Meanwhile, other ethnic groups achieve higher academic scores, in part because they are not wasting time on bilingual classes and culture and failing to master the language of the marketplace and higher education—English. Since there are seldom enough bilingual teachers, Arab, Asian, and European students go right into classes with English-speaking students. They achieve higher scores and more of them graduate than the bilingually taught. The Center for Equal Opportunity in its reports shows the dangers of bilingualism and demands its reform. Otherwise the United States will become deeply divided linguistically and be stuck with a Latin underclass that cannot meet the needs of a high-tech workplace because its English is poor.

*Hispanics . . . taught in bilingual programs test behind peers taught in English-only classrooms, drop out of school at a high rate, and are trapped in . . . low-paying jobs.*

Since Latino immigration—legal or illegal—is likely to continue in the future and since Latino fertility levels are high, the Latino population will grow. According to Hoover economist Edward Lazear, the economic costs of not adequately educating Hispanics will be great, and their economic well-being will be lower than if they were to stay in school longer and focus on English, not on bilingualism. Lazear argues that much of the anti-immigrant rhetoric in America is generated by government policies that reduce the incentives to become assimilated and emphasize the differences among ethnic groups in the population. Examples are bilingual education and unbalanced immigration policies that bring in large numbers of Asians and Hispanics who move into large and stable ghettos.

---

*The old total immersion system still works best; the longer students stay in segregated bilingual programs, the less successful they are in school.*

---

Rosalie Pedalino Porter, a bilingual education teacher for more than twenty years, is convinced that all limited-English-proficiency students can learn English well enough for regular classroom work in one to three years, if given some help. The old total immersion system still works best; the longer students stay in segregated bilingual programs, the less successful they are in school. Even after twenty-eight years of bilingual programs, the dropout rate for Latinos is the highest in the country. In Los Angeles the Latino students dropped out at double the state average (44 percent over four years of high school). Special English-language instruction from day one gets better results than Spanish-language instruction for most of the day.

## Political costs

Latino activists now call for limited recognition to be accorded to Spanish—*inglés y más* ("English and more") runs the slogan. (Official documents of various kinds are now printed in Spanish and other languages as well as English. At the Democratic convention of 1996 speeches were given in Spanish as well as English.) If this course continues, the demand for recognition of Spanish will inevitably change into a demand for recognition of Spanish as an official language. Such a transformation would give great benefits to Spanish speakers in public employment but leave others at a disadvantage. Bilingualism, or multilingualism, imposes economic transaction costs; the political costs are even higher. I do not wish to see the United States become a bilingual country like Canada or Belgium, which both suffer from divisiveness occasioned by the language issue. . . .

I oppose those educators in publicly funded high schools who believe that their task is to maintain the immigrant's cultural heritage. Such endeavors should be left to parents, churches, "Saturday schools," and the extended family. The role of the public schoolteacher is to instruct students in English and American culture and political values. English plays a crucial role in cultural assimilation, a proposition evident also to minority people. (In Brooklyn, for example, the Bushwick Parents Organization went to court in 1996 to oppose the Spanish-English education of Hispanics in the local public schools, arguing that this instruction would leave their children badly disadvantaged when they graduated.) As Ruth Wisse, herself a distinguished educator, puts it, before we encourage ethnic-language revivals in the European manner, "we should recall what millions of immigrants instinctively grasped: that English is the most fundamental pathway to America's equal opportunities." (The European experience is likewise clear. "In general, mother-tongue education is unrealistic and unsuccessful. The children of immigrant parents rapidly acquire the language of their country of residence, and are often less comfortable and successful in their parents' mother-tongue.")

A Center for Immigration Studies *Backgrounder* (April 1996) asks the question, "Are immigration preferences for English-speakers racist?" The Center answers in the negative because one-third of humanity has some knowledge of the English language and most of these people are nonwhite. Although the 1996 immigration bills in the House and Senate had an English requirement for certain employee-based categories of immigrants, it was removed lest it discriminate against nonwhites.

---

*The federal legislation calling for bilingual education "expired a decade ago," yet bilingual education persists.*

---

Knowledge of English is an acquired, not an inherent, skill—anyone, white, black, or brown, can learn English. Immigrants line up to learn English because they believe that learning English will improve their prospects—and it does, significantly. English is the most widely used language in history. English is the language of science, technology, diplomacy, international trade, and commerce. Half of Europe's business is carried out in English, and more than 66 percent of the world's scientists read English. Eighty percent of the world's electronically stored information is in English. The world's forty million Internet users mostly communicate in English. Experts conclude that one-third of mankind speaks or understands some English. Selecting immigrants on the basis of some command of the language therefore cannot be discriminatory.

## English literacy is key to success

Bilingual education in California is a vast industry—about 1.3 million children attend bilingual classes at a cost of more than $5 billion a year. (In the United States 2.6 million students are enrolled in bilingual classes. There is, therefore, a financial incentive to keeping the system.) Schools that provide bilingual education are able to get numerous federal and state grants. Yet bilingual education is a bizarre and unsuccessful program. Only about 5 percent of children in bilingual classes ever make it into English-speaking classes each year. And large numbers of children, mostly Spanish speakers, leave school unable to read or write English, the official language of their adopted country. Shockingly, the federal legislation calling for bilingual education "expired a decade ago," yet bilingual education persists.

Bilingual education was on the California ballot in 1998, thanks to Silicon Valley entrepreneur Unz. He launched a drive to get 433,000 signatures to put an end to bilingual education in California schools. Some polls show that most Latino parents prefer their children to learn English as soon as possible. They believe, correctly, that English literacy is the key to success in the United States. Bilingual teachers are paid more, and schools with bilingual programs get large grants from federal and state programs. Nevertheless, most studies by independent researchers charge that bilingual education is unnecessary and a failure. Most students never really learn to read or write English well, and Spanish speakers leave school at the highest rate of any ethnic group. Bilingual education also defeats efforts to assimilate children into U.S. society and is against the wish of most parents. The solution, Unz and others insist, is one year of sheltered English immersion, then into regular classrooms. Most people seem to agree except bilingual teachers, administrators, and multiculturists who want not only language training but also cultural maintenance or, in other words, want to create little Quebecs in states like California, New York, Texas, and Florida. The evidence is overwhelming: bilingualism does not work, is expensive, is divisive, and ill serves Spanish speakers to advance and compete in American society.

The "English for the Children" ballot initiative called for stopping the teaching of non-English-speaking children in their mother tongue, unless their parents request it. Instead a year of "sheltered English immersion" should be required before placing them in English-only classrooms. Ron Unz, the initiator of the ballot, also mandates $50 million a year for ten years for adult literacy programs. Although the ballot measure passed, opposition to the new law has already begun at local school levels.

Advocates of bilingual education reluctantly concede the system does not work. But political infighting in the California legislature has prevented rational reform. Large numbers of children each year are forced into bilingual classes even if their parents don't want it. Bilingual teachers, moreover, are in short supply, so some teachers are hired who have no teacher training but speak Spanish or some language other than English. This results in poor teaching and little or no English-language teaching.

# 5

# Two-Way Bilingual Programs Benefit Both English- and Non-English-Speaking Students

## Wayne P. Thomas and Virginia P. Collier

*Wayne P. Thomas is professor of research and evaluation methods at the Graduate School of Education at George Mason University. Virginia P. Collier is professor of bilingual/multicultural/ESL education in the same department and university. The authors are also researchers with the Center for Research on Education, Diversity, and Excellence (CREDE), funded by the U.S. Department of Education Office of Educational Research and Improvement.*

In a two-way bilingual education program, language-minority students and native English speakers receive schooling through each other's languages. For example, native Spanish-speakers and native English-speakers are grouped in a class, where they both learn to speak the two languages proficiently. Such a program uses the students' linguistic and cultural experiences as resources for learning. Both language groups serve as peer tutors to each other, which contributes to a richer interaction among students and, hopefully, mutual respect in later adult life. Dual-language programs have also been found to provide constant stimulus and intellectual challenge to students, which may lead to higher school achievement.

D ual language programs help native and nonnative speakers of English speak two languages proficiently—and they do so in cost-effective ways that lead to high academic achievement for all students.

Among the underachieving youth in U.S. schools, students with no proficiency in English must overcome enormous equity gaps, school achievement tests in English show. Over the past three decades, schools have developed a wide range of programs to serve these English learners.

After much experimentation, U.S. schools now have clear achievement data that point to the most powerful models of effective schooling for English learners. What is astounding is that these same programs are also dynamic models for school reform for all students.

Imagine how the 21st century will look. Our world will surely be in constant change, for we are facing this pattern now. The predictions of the near future also depict an interconnected world, with global travel and instant international communications. Right now, many U.S. businesses seek employees proficient in both English and another language. Students who graduate with monocultural perspectives will not be prepared to contribute to their societies, for cross-cultural contact is at an all-time high in human history as population mobility continues throughout the world. Thus, majority and minority language students together must prepare for a constantly changing world.

## Tapping the power of linguistic diversity

For more than three decades, as we have struggled to develop effective models for schooling English learners, we have mostly considered the choices available to us from a deficit perspective. That is, we have often viewed English learners as a "problem" for our schools (oh, no—they don't know English), and so we "remediate" by sending them to a specialist to be "fixed." In the remedial programs, English learners receive less access to the standard grade-level curriculum. The achievement and equity gap increases as native English speakers forge ahead while English learners make less progress. Thus, underachieving groups continue to underachieve in the next generation. Unfortunately, the two most common types of U.S. school services provided for English learners—English as a Second Language (ESL) pullout and transitional bilingual education—are remedial in nature. Participating students and teachers suffer often from the social consequences of this perception.

But when the focus of any special school program is on academic enrichment for all students, the school community perceives that program positively, and students become academically successful and deeply engaged in the learning process. Thus, enrichment programs for English learners are extremely effective when they are intellectually challenging and use students' linguistic and cultural experiences as a resource for interdisciplinary discovery learning. Further, educators who use the enrichment models that were initially developed for English learners are beginning to see the power of these models for all students.

## A history of bilingual enrichment

These innovative enrichment models are called by varying names:—dual language, bilingual immersion, two-way bilingual, and developmental bilingual education. We recommend these models as forms of mainstream education through two languages that will benefit all students. Let's examine the history of their development and some basic characteristics of these models.

Initially, the first two 20th-century experiments with bilingual education in the United States and Canada in the early 1960s came about as a result of parental pressure. Both of these experiments were enrichment models. In Canada, English-speaking parents who wanted their children to develop deep proficiency in both French and English initiated what became known as immersion education. Immersion is a commitment to bilingual schooling throughout grades K-12 in which students are instructed 90 percent of the school day during kindergarten and grade 1 in the minority language chosen for the program, and 10 percent of the day in the majority language (English). The hands-on nature of academic work in the early grades is a natural vehicle for proficiency development of the minority language.

Immersion programs emphasize the less dominant language more than English in the first years, because the minority language is less supported by the broader society, and academic uses of the language are less easily acquired outside school. Gradually, with each subsequent grade, the program provides more instruction in the majority language until children learn the curriculum equally through both languages by grade 4 or 5. By grade 6, students have generally developed deep academic proficiency in both languages, and they can work on math, science, social studies, and language arts at or above grade level in either language. From the 1960s to the 1990s, immersion bilingual schooling has grown immensely popular in Canada and has achieved high rates of success with majority and minority students, students of middle- and low-income families, as well as students with learning disabilities.

> *Enrichment programs . . . are extremely effective when they . . . use students' linguistic and cultural experiences as a resource.*

About the same time that the first immersion program started in Canada, Cubans arriving in Miami, Florida, initiated the first U.S. experiment with two-way bilingual education in 1963. The term two-way refers to two language groups acquiring the curriculum through each other's languages; one-way bilingual education refers to one language group receiving schooling through two languages. Intent on overthrowing Fidel Castro and returning to their country, the Cuban arrivals established private bilingual schools to develop their children's English and maintain their Spanish. The public schools, losing significant enrollment, chose to develop bilingual classes to attract students back. As English-speaking parents enrolled their children in the classes, two-way, integrated bilingual schooling emerged as a new program model in the United States. These classes provided a half day of the grade-level curriculum in Spanish and a half day in English, now known as the 50-50 model of two-way.

Over time, these two experiments have expanded to many states in the United States as school communities recognize the benefits for all students. The immersion model, originally developed in Canada for majority language speakers, has become known as the 90-10 two-way model in the United States because during the first two years both language groups receive 90 percent of the instruction through the minority language.

Key to the success of all two-way programs is the fact that both language groups stay together throughout the school day, serving as peer tutors for each other. Peer models stimulate natural language acquisition for both groups because they keep the level of interaction cognitively complex. Research has consistently demonstrated that academic achievement is very high for all groups of participants compared to control groups who receive schooling only through English. This holds true for students of low socioeconomic status, as well as African-American students and language-minority students, with those in the 90-10 model achieving even higher than those in the 50-50 model.

## The role of careful planning

What are other essential characteristics of this school reform? An important principle is clear curricular separation of the two languages of instruction. To maintain a continuous cognitive challenge, teachers do not repeat or translate lessons in the second language, but reinforce concepts taught in one language across the two languages in a spiraling curriculum. Teachers alternate the language of instruction by theme or subject area, by time of day, by day of the week, or by the week. If two teachers are teaming, each teacher represents one language. When two teachers share and exchange two classes, this is a cost-effective, mainstream model that adds no additional teachers to a school system's budget. In contrast, ESL pull-out is the most costly of all program models for English learners because extra ESL resource teachers must be added to the mainstream staff.

Successful two-way bilingual education includes
- a minimum of six years of bilingual instruction;
- focus on the core academic curriculum rather than on a watered-down version;
- quality language arts instruction in both languages;
- separation of the two languages for instruction;
- use of the non-English language for at least 50 percent of the instructional time and as much as 90 percent in the early grades;
- an additive bilingual environment that has full support of school administrators;
- a balanced ratio of students who speak each language (for example, 50:50 or 60:40, preferably not to go below 70:30);
- promotion of positive interdependence among peers and between teachers and students;
- high-quality instructional personnel; and
- active parent-school partnerships.

Demographics influence the feasibility of two-way programs, because the students in each language group serve as peer teachers for each other. A natural choice for many U.S. schools is a Spanish-English two-way program, because Spanish speakers are most often the largest language group. In the 204 two-way bilingual schools identified in the United States in a 1997 survey, other languages of instruction in addition to Spanish include, in order of frequency, Korean, French, Cantonese, Navajo, Japanese, Arabic, Portuguese, Russian, and Mandarin Chinese.

What makes these programs work? To answer this question, let's look at the students who are initially the lowest achievers on tests in English. Most school policymakers commonly assume that students need only a couple of years to learn a second language. But while these students make dramatic progress in English development in the first two years, English language learners are competing with a moving target, the native English speaker, when tested in English.

The average native English speaker typically gains 10 months of academic growth in one 10-month school year in English development because first language acquisition is a natural work in progress throughout the school years, not completed until young adulthood. Although some score higher and some lower, on average they also make a year's progress in a year's time in mathematics, science, and social studies. Thus students not yet proficient in English initially score three or more years below grade level on the tests in English because they cannot yet demonstrate in their second language all that they actually know. These students must outgain the native speaker by making one and one-half years' progress on the academic tests in their second language for each of six successive school years (a total of nine years progress in six years) to reach the typical performance level of the constantly advancing native English speaker.

When students do academic work in their primary language for more than two to three years (the typical support time in a transitional bilingual program), they are able to demonstrate with each succeeding year that they are making more gains than the native English speaker—and closing the gap in achievement as measured by tests in English across the curriculum. After five to six years of enrichment bilingual schooling, former English learners (now proficient in English) are able to demonstrate their deep knowledge on the academic tests in English across the curriculum, as well as in their native language, achieving on or above grade level.

## Bridging the gap to a better tomorrow

Why is such progress for English learners important for our schools? Language-minority students are predicted to account for about 40 percent of the school-age population by the 2030s. It is in our pragmatic self-interest to ensure their success as young adults, for they will be key to a robust economy to pay retirement and medical benefits for today's working adults. We must close the equity gap by providing enrichment schooling for all. For native English speakers as well as language-minority students, the enrichment bilingual classes appear to provide a constant stimulus and intellectual challenge similar to that of a gifted and talented class. The research evidence is overwhelmingly clear that proficient bilinguals outperform monolinguals on school tests. Crossing cultural, social class, and language boundaries, students in a bilingual class develop multiple ways of solving human problems and approach ecological and social science issues from a crossnational perspective. These learners acquire deep academic proficiency in two languages, which becomes a valuable resource in adult professional life. And they learn to value each other's knowledge and life experiences—leading to meaningful respect and collaboration that lasts a lifetime.

# 6

# English-Only Education Should Be Standard in Most Schools

## Ron K. Unz

*Ron K. Unz, a Silicon Valley businessman, is at the forefront of the movement called English for the Children, which aims to teach school children in English only. He launched, led, and financed Proposition 227, a ballot initiative approved by California voters in 1998 that sought to end bilingual education in schools. Since then, he has brought the campaign to other states, with the goal of dismantling bilingual education throughout the country.*

*[Editor's note: The following viewpoint was written in January 1998, several months prior to the passage of Proposition 227 in California.]*

English is today's international language, dominating science, technology, and global business. For this reason, English literacy is very important. It is therefore ironic that in many schools in America, English is not taught to children as they start their schooling. Bilingual education has produced dismal results. Of the 1.3 million children who begin each year without knowing English, only about 5 percent learn English by year's end. Bilingual education should be abandoned in most schools, and English-only education should be the norm.

As each new microchip and fiber-optic cable shrinks the circumference of our world, more and more Americans recognize the practical importance of bilingualism. Even today, entrepreneurs or employees fluent in Chinese, Japanese or Spanish have a distinct edge over their English-only peers.

But if other languages such as Chinese or Spanish are of growing world importance, English ranks in a class by itself. Although English is not and never has been America's official national language, over the past twenty years it has rapidly become the entire world's unofficial interna-

Ron K. Unz, "'Bilingual Education' Ineffective Initiative: Schools Harm Spanish-Speaking Kids by Not Teaching English," www.gseis.ucla.edu, January 16, 1998. Copyright © 1997 by Graduate School of Education and Information Studies, University of California, Los Angeles. Reproduced by permission.

tional language, utterly dominating the spheres of science, technology and international business. Fluency in Spanish may provide a significant advantage, but lack of literacy in English represents a crippling, almost fatal disadvantage in our global economy. For this reason, the better public and private schools in Europe, Asia and Latin America all provide as much English as early as possible to young children.

## Inspired by multiculturalist ideology

During this same period, many of America's own public schools have stopped teaching English to young children from non-English-speaking backgrounds. Influenced by avant-garde pedagogy and multiculturalist ideology, educational administrators have adopted a system of bilingual education that is usually "bilingual" in name only.

Too often, young immigrant children are taught little or no English—in Los Angeles, only thirty minutes a day, according to the school district's long-standing bilingual master plan. This is based on the ridiculous notion that too much English too early will damage a child's self-esteem and learning ability. Hundreds of thousands of these American schoolchildren spend years being taught grammar, reading, writing and all other academic subjects in their own "native" language—almost always Spanish—while receiving just tiny doses of instruction in English which is taught as a foreign language.

---

*Lack of literacy in English represents a crippling, almost fatal disadvantage in our global economy.*

---

As one might expect, the results of such an approach to English instruction are utterly dismal. Of the 1.3 million California schoolchildren (a quarter of our state's total public school enrollment) who begin each year classified as not knowing English, only about five percent learn English by year's end, implying an annual failure rate of 95 percent for existing programs.

Defenders of the status quo argue away these devastating statistics by claiming that 5-year-old children normally require about seven years to learn a new language and actually have much more difficulty learning second languages than teenagers or adults; these are academic dogmas with absolutely no basis in reality.

On the other hand, the dreadful flaws in the current classification methodology are kept well hidden. In California, children from immigrant or Latino backgrounds are categorized as not knowing English if they merely score below average on English tests, meaning that unknown numbers of children whose first and only language is English spend their elementary school years trapped in Spanish-only "bilingual" programs.

## Special government funding

The real dynamic driving this bizarre system is special government funding. School districts are provided with extra dollars for each child who doesn't know English. This generates the worst sort of perverse incentive in which administrators are financially rewarded for not teaching English to young children or pretending that they haven't learned the language; schools are annually penalized for each child who becomes fluent in English.

Under such a scheme, the widespread educational myth that young children require seven years to learn English suddenly becomes understandable as a necessary, enabling myth. And although no one has been able to properly document the total amount of supplemental spending on children limited in English, the annual total for California certainly exceeds $400 million and probably exceeds $1 billion, sums that can buy a tremendous amount of silence or complicity.

> *"Bilingual education" is completely unworkable as well as unsuccessful.*

Unfortunately for its profiteers, "bilingual education" is completely unworkable as well as unsuccessful. Even after twenty or thirty years of effort, California has had absolutely no luck in finding the enormous supply of properly certified bilingual teachers to match the 140 languages spoken by California schoolchildren. All sides in the debate agree that the old-fashioned "sink or swim" method of learning English is the worst alternative.

However, today more California schoolchildren are submerged into this approach than are placed in properly structured bilingual programs, although courts have ruled the former unconstitutional and the latter legally mandatory. "Bilingual or nothing" in practice often means "nothing."

These facts may only now be coming to the attention of California's affluent white elite, but they have been well-known to the current system's primary victims, powerless Latino immigrants and their children. . . .

Our initiative [Proposition 227] which has now [inspired other states] would end bilingual education in California by making it truly voluntary.

## Bilingual programs should be strictly voluntary

Parents could still have their children placed or kept in a bilingual program, but only if they took the affirmative step of seeking a waiver. Since public opinion surveys, including a recent Los Angeles Times poll, have consistently shown 80 percent to 85 percent dislike for the current program among its supposed beneficiaries, voluntary bilingual programs will become very few and far between. And those programs that do survive our initiative by attracting genuine parental support are probably worth preserving. In a state as large and diverse as California, even the most unlikely program may occasionally succeed due to specific local conditions or unique individuals.

But either way, all of California's immigrant schoolchildren finally will be granted the right to be taught English, the universal language of advancement and opportunity, supplementing their own family languages. Only by ending our failed system of bilingual education can we foster the true growth of bilingualism and the unity and prosperity of our multiethnic society.

# 7

# English-Only Education Ignores Social and Political Realities

## Jill Kerper Mora

*Jill Kerper Mora is a professor of education at San Diego State University in California.*

Proposition 227 was passed by a majority of California voters in 1998 to ban bilingual education and the use of languages other than English for instruction in public schools. The assumption of the new law is that American culture is being endangered by allowing school children to use their native languages. Proposition 227 ignores the fact that bilingualism thrives in California: More than one-third of the population speaks a language other than English at home. Also, opponents of bilingualism fail to recognize that most Spanish-speakers assimilate successfully—within two generations—into American culture.

On June 2, 1998 a 61% majority of California voters elected to impose an English-only ideology on the public schools by passing Proposition 227. This law was the "English for the Children" initiative that banned bilingual education and the use of languages other than English for instruction in the public schools. Proposition 227 reverses policies set in place in 1967 by then Governor Ronald Reagan that allowed bilingual instruction as one option for addressing providing limited English proficient students equal access to the school curriculum. The changes in the education code stemming from Proposition 227 have brought court action by the Mexican American Legal Defense and Education Fund (MALDEF) and other civil rights groups, claiming that the law violates the rights of language minority students to an equal education.

Proposition 227 was passed following a campaign sponsored and financed by Official English and other English-only advocates. These groups claimed that bilingual education poses a threat to the homogeneity of American culture. The campaign was filled with extreme rhetoric that

Jill Kerper Mora, "Debunking English-Only Ideology: Bilingual Educators Are Not the Enemy," http://coe.sdsu.edu, October 23, 2002. Copyright © 2002 by Jill Kerper Mora. Reproduced by permission.

painted bilingual educators as "ethnic militants" and "Hispanic separatists" who were harming language minority students by denying them the opportunity to learn English. Even the more benign arguments by the supporters of Proposition 227 characterized bilingual teachers and administrators as mercenaries who were putting their pocketbooks before the best interests of children in a battle to keep state funding for bilingual programs.

Proposition 227 includes provisions that school officials and teachers can be sued for personal liability and damages for failing to implement the English-only provisions of the law. This extreme policy is based on the assumption that resistance to elimination of bilingual programs would occur based on a rebellious desire to maintain minority cultural values and language use, even though the electorate finds this goal objectionable. The effect that this provision and the mandates of Proposition 227 have within the educational community is to ensure that minority educators will be marginalized in decision making in the design and implementation of programs that serve minority students.

## Demographic realities

We must examine the assumptions of the English-only ideology, especially as they apply to today's social and educational realities. California is a state with great linguistic and cultural diversity. A survey released by the U.S. Census Bureau and reported in the San Diego Union Tribune (Sánchez, 2001, November 24) is testimony to the prevalence of bilingualism in California. One out of every four California residents (26%) was born outside the United States and more than one third of the population (38.6%) speaks a language other than English in the home. These statistics are mirrored by an equal proportion (25%) of public school students who are classified as limited in English proficiency (LEP) and fully 38% of all California's public school students who speak a native language other than English. One out of every three students is a Spanish/English bilingual learner. Most of these Californians learn to speak English fluently and become fully assimilated, or Americanized, within two generations. Oftentimes, third generation Mexican Americans cannot communicate in Spanish with their grandparents. However, more and more Hispanics today are preserving their bilingual skills because of their continued familial and economic ties to their countries of origin and because of the advantages of being bilingual.

---

*One out of every three students [in California] is a Spanish/English bilingual learner.*

---

A recent study by the Strategy Research Corporation of Hispanic households throughout the United States found that 64% of Hispanics are equally proficient and comfortable using Spanish and English. Assimilation into American culture is driven by economic and social factors that have little to do with what language minorities learn, or fail to learn, in public schools.

In spite of the realities of rapid assimilation, advocates of English-only have convinced a portion of the electorate that unless school children are denied the use of their native languages for learning to read and write and studying academic subjects, American culture is endangered. They believe that the greatest threat comes from granting equal status to other languages, predominantly Spanish, in a publicly funded institution such as public schools. English-only advocates claim that giving minority educators decision-making authority over programs and policies in schools and classroom constitutes a threat to the power of monolingual teachers, the true representatives of American cultural values. The assumption, which borders on paranoid, is that bilingual educators must be legally restrained because their motives and loyalties are suspect. Proposition 227 protects the power of monolingual teachers to decide how language minority students will be educated, without having to consider the opinions and values of their bilingual colleagues who have expertise in language education.

Wayne Cornelius and Ruben Rumbaut with the UCSD Center for U.S.-Mexico studies (1995) found that there are three distinct patterns of assimilation for new arrivals from Mexico and Latin America. One out of every four foreign-born Americans is from Mexico. One pattern (Group 1) is comprised of new arrivals to the United States who join the large Latino communities in the urban areas like Los Angeles, often prospering there as part of the community's economic and social life. These Latinos tend to become bilingual, but often learn English only to the extent that it serves their instrumental and practical needs. The bulk of their lives are lived within the Spanish-speaking community. Their children tend to also become bilingual in school and remain so, not losing their Spanish because it has enormous practical benefits and is constantly being refreshed by new arrivals.

---

*The negative impact of policies that seek to promote English fluency at any cost . . . [include the] loss of other languages and the sacrifice of valuable linguistic skills.*

---

The second pattern (Group 2) is comprised of Latinos who become part of the Anglo middle class, usually a gradual process that is completed by the second or third generation. These Latinos tend to lose their Spanish and sever their ties to their homeland.

The third pattern (Group 3) is the most worrisome—assimilation into an almost permanent underclass. These Latino youths tend to reject their Mexican roots and rebel against their parents' cultural and linguistic values. They become monolingual English speakers, but not proficient enough or well enough educated in English to advance into the middle class. They get the poorest level of schooling and often live in separate ghetto-like communities, often isolated from both the vibrant Latino community and the Anglo community.

Assimilation means something very different to each of these groups. This explains the range of opinion on issues such as bilingual education among Latinos. Many of the members of Group 2 (middle-class, assimilated) tend to say, "We did it. Why can't they?" The answer is that strong economic and educational factors determine which group the new arrivals fall into. For Group 1, the idea of assimilation, certainly as conservatives understand it, is almost beside the point. They distrust the concept and its supporters out of fear that it means pressure to give up their ties to Latin America and their Spanish as a resource for economic advancement. For Group 3, the concept of assimilation is an empty promise. They got the brutal end of the "brutal bargain" by sacrificing their cultural identity and ties to the Spanish-speaking community, getting nothing in return.

## The second generation

In an outstandingly thorough and clearly written book by Alejandro Portes and Ruben Rumbaut (2001) titled "Legacies: The Story of the Immigrant Second Generation" these sociologists fully describe the experiences of immigrant youth in the acculturation process. Portes is at Princeton and Rumbaut is at Michigan State. They have done a masterful job of clarifying the issues surrounding Proposition 227, bilingual education and immigrant students.

Portes and Rumbaut document the clear advantages in school achievement among "fluent bilinguals" as opposed to immigrant children who are "English-dominant" or "limited bilinguals." They describe the negative impact of policies that seek to promote English fluency at any cost, including the stigmatization and loss of other languages and the sacrifice of valuable linguistic skills, as well as an increasing distance from parents because of the implicit message to children that they are carriers of an inferior culture. According to Portes and Rumbaut, "*. . .forced English immersion promotes dissonant acculturation with negative consequences that can far exceed the alleged benefits of such programs.*"

---

*Coercive policies do not increase the rate of acculturation of immigrants.*

---

These authors explain three distinct patterns of social integration among first and second generation immigrants based on background factors, intergenerational patterns and external obstacles. Each of these patterns yields different expected outcomes. Dissonant acculturation occurs when immigrants confront discrimination where the messages about one's culture and language are negative and demeaning. It leads to "downward assimilation" where immigrants become "trapped" into lower socioeconomic, often segregated, communities and may lead to adversarial attitudes and lifestyles. Dissonant acculturation results in a pessimistic view of the individual's opportunities for upward mobility and diminished ambition and aspirations to become part of mainstream society.

Contrarily, consonant and selective acculturation occur when external obstacles to assimilation are met with family support and countervailing messages about the value of the individual and his or her language and culture. Selective acculturation occurs when messages of exclusion and discrimination are filtered through ethnic networks and confronted with the help of family and community resources and support that enhance ambition and higher aspirations through various modes of social incorporation. Selective acculturation results in upward assimilation combined with biculturalism.

"Forced march assimilation" policies that attempt to use the public schools to wipe out bilingualism such as California's Proposition 227 and Arizona's Proposition 203 produce resistance and resentment from ethnic communities that result in more segregation and encapsulation, and thus more "dissonant acculturation." Today's immigrants from Mexico, Latin America and the Caribbean are very different from the immigrants who arrived on Ellis Island in the early part of the century. The social and economic motivations for immigrants to become integrated into American society and to learn English are very strong. These will not be weakened by acceptance of bilingualism and biculturalism in our society. However, prejudice and discrimination against immigrants who choose bilingualism over English monolingualism is damaging because it results in policies that are exclusionary and counterproductive. We must as a nation be open to new modes of acculturation or risk exacerbating rather than ameliorating the challenges of our diversity.

The authors point out that "*. . . from a long-term perspective, policies toward Mexican immigration advocated by the two mainstream ideologies . . . verge on the suicidal*" because of the demand for Mexican labor and the heavy discrimination that result in impoverished barrios of the major urban areas. They speak eloquently about the need to enlighten the "white middle-class electorate", the "dominant majority" as to "where its real self-interests lie in the long run and thus, build a constituency for an alternative set of policies." Portes and Rumbaut make an excellent case for the urgency of this effort for the future of our urban centers where immigrants concentrate and for American society as a whole. . . .

Portes and Rumbaut discuss the contrasts between the ideology underlying Proposition 187, which they describe as "intransigent nativism" in contrast with proponents of "forceful assimilation" embodied in Proposition 227. They say this:

> Despite being grounded on thoughtful reflection on immigration history, Unz's Proposition 227 is designed to accomplish exactly the opposite. Despite its moderation, its vision is ultimately reactionary. It wants an America as it was in the 1920's, a relatively isolated society, not as it must be in the new millennium, after it successfully emerged as the core of the global system. In the process, old-line assimilationism undermines the very forces of parental authority and ambition that can overcome the barriers to successful adaptation and forge productive and self-respecting citizens out of the new second generation.

We language minority educators agree with this assessment of the challenges posed by high levels of immigration. What is born out by the research is that coercive policies do not increase the rate of acculturation of immigrants, and in many ways work against the very kind of consonant and selective acculturation that produce upward assimilation and integration of immigrants with each successive generation. We have much more to fear from policies that send the message that immigrants must renounce their language and culture and attempt to coerce assimilation than we have to fear from immigrant communities that are bilingual and bicultural.

## Ideological litmus test

When viewed critically, it is apparent that the English-only ideology is nothing more than an elevated conspiracy theory based on negative stereotypes about bilingual and bicultural individuals. To those who believe that restrictions on the use of other languages in public schools, bilingualism implies divided allegiance to conflicting cultural values and competing lifestyles. Bilingual educators have been unfairly and needlessly portrayed as espousing beliefs and practices that undermine children's assimilation into American culture when they cast other languages and cultures in a positive light. They have been accused of being "hostile to English" because they wish to maintain bilingual instruction in the public school. A rejection of a belief in bilingual education has become an ideological "litmus test" of language loyalty for educators in the climate created by the English-only movement during the campaign for Proposition 227.

> *The . . . monolingual population . . . has deliberately chosen to mobilize around English as a symbol in order to revive a one-nation-one-language principle.*

Guadalupe Valdés (1997) makes some excellent points that illuminate the controversy over bilingual education. First, she points out that in the United States the dominant, monolingual population that has deliberately chosen to mobilize around English as a symbol in order to revive a one-nation-one-language principle. We must consider how minimal and reasonable the minority's demands for rights to bilingual education have always been and really how little the majority population is asked to give up to allow it to continue. In fact, transitional bilingual education has always involved using Spanish as a means to an end rather than having the status of being an end in itself. Yet, even this appears to be too much for the dominant group to tolerate. Valdés goes on to say this:

> . . . policies—no matter how benevolent in intention or how naively ignorant—that treat groups of human beings unjustly are policies that ultimately violate the individual human rights of those persons who share the particular characteristics to which the policy in question does not attend. In the case of bilingual individuals . . . policies enacted for monolinguals by monolingual individuals inevitably deprive members of bilingual populations of essential human rights that no state can be justified in restricting or violating.

Bilingual education is something that the minority wants, but the majority seems not to want them to have it. This is not because they want it for themselves, because for the most part they don't. They simply want to make sure that the minority doesn't have it. Since the minority benefits from bilingual education and it really does no harm to the majority for them to have it, I believe that ultimately it will be the majority that must concede on this issue. So, ultimately it is a question of who must give in. If the minority is made to give in, its real and tangible loss is very great. If the majority gives in, it loses nothing and gains an indirect benefit by supporting and accommodating the minority. . . .

Since language is a means of communication and the reproduction of a collective identity, language rights are difficult to define and defend as individual rights. Therefore, we must argue that there are collective linguistic rights at stake in the battle against 227 and 203 that must gain legal recognition and protection under our Constitution. Valdés (1997) argues that one of these rights is for language minority school children to have access to adults committed to understanding and addressing their unique educational problems (i.e., bilingual teachers, administrators, etc.).

## The realities of bilingualism

The reality of bilingualism is contrary to the myth of English-only. Most bilingual individuals live very comfortably within their different cultural milieus, without conflicts or stress. In fact, they experience an enriched lifestyle that incorporates diverse customs and traditions. Bilingual educators are individuals who have achieved the benefits of two languages and cultures. They are professionals who have achieved high levels of status in American society, benefiting from the diversity in their backgrounds. Their language skills and cultural knowledge should be valued rather than denigrated in these times of diversity and change in the demographic make-up of California. This is especially compelling when we consider the fact that Spanish is the third most widely spoken language in the world. Spanish is spoken in 28 countries around the globe. The United States has the sixth largest Spanish-speaking population of any country in the world.

> *Bilingualism is growing because of strong economic and cultural factors that are far beyond the scope of the public schools.*

In reality, bilingualism is growing because of strong economic and cultural factors that are far beyond the scope of the public schools. One of these elements is trade with Latin America. Mexico is California's number one trading partner, with $15 billion annually in goods and services exchanged between the two. Along with this amount of trade, there is the inevitable and mutually beneficial exchange of cultures. Spanish/English bilingual skills take on a high commercial value and give a competitive edge to workers in this interdependent economy. There are many families, and even communities, that maintain what is called a "transnational" lifestyle, with frequent exchanges and travel between their country of origin and the United States. This phenomenon is common with immigrants living along the U.S.A-Mexico border, for example.

Bilingualism is an asset, and often a requirement, for supervisors and managers who work with a largely Spanish-speaking workforce in business and industry. Although English-only restrictions are frequently imposed in work environments, these rules are largely ineffective. Such policies are often merely a statement about power relationships within the business and are counter-productive, or even dangerous, in accomplishing their purposes. Rather than create respect for higher management and an adherence to an exclusive use of English, these restrictions damage relationships with workers and cause resistance among workers to management's "authority."

## Linguistic freedom in a democratic society

The English-only ideology is actually in contradiction with what it truly means to be an American. Proponents of language restrictions as public policy demonstrate a lack of faith in the power of American democratic ideals of social justice and equality to unite us in a common purpose, despite our differences. Individual freedoms and the guarantee of rights under our Constitution transcend our cultural and linguistic origins and practices. We should not brand bilingual educators as separatists or cultural subversives because they believe that children can be taught effectively in their native language while they learn English. In reality, we should respect their expertise and defer to their commitment to language-minority students' effective education.

Fair-minded and intellectually honest voters and those who are genuinely concerned about equal educational opportunities for all students must reject the demonization of bilingual educators by the English-only movement to gain a political advantage and win supporters. Bilingual educators are in fact cultural mediators who facilitate the assimilation of language minority students, provided they do not work under the threat of legal liabilities for exercising their professional judgments. The unifying principles of American democracy must not be set aside in the name of a forced linguistic unification of our diverse society. Such an ideology is the real enemy of American culture.

# 8

# English Immersion Has Led to Higher Test Scores

## Ken Noonan

*Ken Noonan is superintendent of schools in Oceanside, California. In 1970, he founded the California Association of Bilingual Educators (CABE), which for years actively campaigned for bilingual education. But after the adoption of Proposition 227 in California in 1998, he became convinced that English immersion is a better approach than bilingual education.*

For many years, bilingual education was the preferred strategy of the Oceanside school district in San Diego, California. However, things changed with the passage of Proposition 227, which mandated schools to teach limited-English speakers in a structured English immersion classroom for one year before moving them to a mainstream class. After one year of implementing English immersion, the district achieved amazing results in English-administered state tests. Specifically, Spanish-speaking students achieved dramatic academic gains in reading and writing, where the district had reduced class size to twenty and implemented phonics reading instruction. Limited-English second graders, taught only in English, scored at the thirty-second percentile on a scale of one hundred in 2000, compared to thirteenth in 1998.

Ivan, a second-grader, sat next to me with a children's book of literature in his lap. Methodically, he ran his index finger along the lines of print and pronounced the words aloud almost flawlessly. Patiently, wanting to finish his assignment, he tolerated my questions designed to test his understanding of what he had read. He understood everything.

"So what?" you may think. Shouldn't second-graders be able to read at grade level? But Ivan, the son of Mexican immigrants, had come to school not quite two years earlier, able to speak and understand only Spanish. The book he was reading and my questions were all in English.

For 30 years, I worked hard to promote bilingual education as the best way for children like Ivan to become academically successful. Two years ago, I campaigned against California's Proposition 227, the ballot measure to eliminate bilingual education, because I believed that it was going to harm Spanish-speaking students. I was certain that students would be confused in English-only instruction and would be lost in the shuffle. I now realize I was wrong.

In June 1998, 61 percent of California voters approved 227, which requires that all students be taught "overwhelmingly" in English and that children who are not proficient in English be taught for at least one year in a structured English-immersion classroom before being assigned to a mainstream class.

Two months later, we began the school year with all classes taught in English. I was nervous, certain that it was going to be a disaster. Since then, however, I've watched Ivan and other recent immigrant children in my district learn to speak and read English faster than I ever thought possible. As a result, I've become convinced that English immersion, not traditional bilingual education, is the path to academic success for children who arrive in our classrooms unable to learn in English.

## Delayed development of English language skills

Even before 227, I had begun to question the effectiveness of traditional bilingual education, in which limited speakers of English are assigned to a class where they learn to speak, read and write in their home language first. In Oceanside, which is 35 miles north of San Diego, that language is Spanish. Until 1998, a student would remain in Spanish instruction for up to four years, even longer for some. Only after being designated fluent in English would a child's learning in English begin in earnest.

As a former bilingual teacher, administrator, and co-founder of the California Association of Bilingual Educators, I had come to believe that many students remained too long in classes conducted in Spanish, and that, as a result, they lost ground in the development of their English language skills. I believe that this creates a learning gap that is seldom closed.

---

*I've become convinced that English immersion . . . is the path to academic success.*

---

On my recommendation, the Oceanside School Board adopted a bilingual program reform that would have moved most students from Spanish to English within three years. But before we could implement that change, 227 was passed. At first, I resisted. I tried every way I could to find some way to preserve bilingual instruction. But I could not, I learned after consulting with the school district's lawyers. In the end, we had no choice but to implement 227 fully and immediately. Reluctantly, I made preparations.

At the end of the first year, I was amazed by the results. State tests showed dramatic academic gains for Spanish-speaking students in reading and writing—especially in the early grades, where we had reduced class size to 20 or fewer students and implemented phonics reading instruction. Those changes seemed to have made a difference.

But Proposition 227 has been the catalyst for the dramatic changes in student achievement. Without 227, we would have been teaching these students in Spanish; they would certainly have performed poorly on the state tests, which are administered in English. And we never would have seen how quickly and how early they could learn to read English.

Consider this: Two years ago, limited-English second-graders in Oceanside scored at the 13th percentile on a scale of 100. This year, at the same grade, limited-English students scored at the 32nd percentile. A significant difference, I believe, is that these students had been taught only in English.

Skeptics claim that Oceanside's scores are so low that they offer scant proof that English immersion works better than bilingual instruction. Oceanside, with 22,000 students in 24 schools, was the lowest-scoring school district in San Diego County for many years. But that is no longer true. The test results of Spanish-speaking students in other districts have risen as well, but at the primary level, no district has seen increases as dramatic as Oceanside's. For the first time, more than half of our schools are at or above the national average in some categories. In reading, our second grade limited-English students' test scores were almost 40 percentage points below the national average two years ago. Today, they are only 18 points from the national average.

---

*English immersion . . . should begin on a student's first day of school.*

---

Critics say that 227 is unclear in its description of how students should be taught. Not so, in my opinion. Simply stated, it requires that all students be taught in English. Parents may request a waiver that would allow them to move their children to a bilingual program. As part of their request, they must list the educational or emotional problems that English immersion would cause their children. The waiver must be approved unless the school staff thinks that it would not be in the child's best interest. A child must spend at least one month in the immersion class before a waiver request can be considered. The district must form a bilingual class when there are 20 or more students with approved waivers at one grade level.

I grew up in Montebello, Calif., in a family where both sides are descended from Irish and Mexican immigrants. My parents, several of my grandparents, my great-grandparents, and all of my aunts and uncles were bilingual in English and Spanish. My sisters and I grew up using both languages interchangeably with our extended family. As a result, I deeply valued bilingualism. And I believed that bilingual education was the best way to achieve this, by preserving the child's native language while teaching him English. That's why I originally opposed 227 as misguided and drastic.

## Students are learning quickly and well

But I was wrong on two counts. First, 227 did not cause the sky to fall in. The children, for the most part, are learning quickly and well. Second, I was wrong in believing that teaching limited-English students to read first in Spanish and later, sometimes much later, in English, would deliver on our promise of academic success. In fact, I have come to believe that transitioning limited-English students to English well after their peers puts those students at an academic disadvantage when it comes to choosing the most challenging courses in high school and college.

Soon after Oceanside schools implemented English-immersion instruction, I was invited to speak with some Hispanic students at our local community college about the new approach. I was criticized and castigated by most of the students, all of whom were advocates of bilingual instruction. I explained my concern about the achievement gap that appears to develop between native English speakers and limited-English speakers who are taught to read, write and speak Spanish in school first. Two female students said little, but after the meeting adjourned they asked to speak with me privately. We found an empty classroom, and they began to question me about my "gap" theory. I made clear that this was merely my opinion and that little research had been done to support my belief.

An awkward silence followed. Finally one, then the other, spoke. Each, they explained, had come to the United States as the children of Spanish-speaking immigrants, and they had been in bilingual classes in two different school districts (one in Oceanside). Both said they felt less proficient in English than their native English-speaking peers in high school and were struggling in college. They had enjoyed being taught in Spanish in public schools, but both now believed that they had paid a price for the comfort of early Spanish instruction.

They asked me if English immersion would help other students like them. I confessed that I did not know. They apologized for the behavior of their classmates, and we said our goodbyes.

That was two years ago. Now I am convinced that English immersion does work and that it should begin on a student's first day of school. Now I believe that English immersion may be able to reduce or eliminate that gap in achievement. Now I believe that using all of the resources of public education to move these students into the English-speaking mainstream early and quickly is far more important than my former romantic notions that preserving the child's home language should be the ultimate goal of our schools.

# 9

# English Immersion Has Not Been Proven to Raise Test Scores

## Kenji Hakuta

*Kenji Hakuta, a professor of education at Stanford University, is a scholar and educator at the forefront of bilingual education and has written extensively on the subject. He is the author of* Mirror of Language: the Debate on Bilingualism, *co-author (with Ellen Bialystok) of* In Other Words: The Science and Psychology of Second-Language Acquisition, *and editor (with Diane August) of* The Debate on Bilingualism, Improving Schooling for Language Minority Children: A Research Agenda.

Pronouncements that English-only approaches work, as shown by increases in test scores in California in 2000, is premature. A high-profile case is that of Oceanside. In 2000, students in the district managed to achieve scores which were higher than scores in past years. However, in 2001, scores in Oceanside stalled. It is too early to derive conclusions from recent measurements of the effects of English-only approaches. School reforms take time to demonstrate their effectiveness. The focus now should be on avoiding rigid prescriptions like Proposition 227, which effectively outlaws bilingual approaches.

[I]n 2000], when state education test results were released in California, we heard a lot about the miracle at Oceanside. Ron K. Unz, the author of Proposition 227 that banned bilingual education in favor of English immersion, crowed about results that showed dramatic gains in reading and math scores—for example a 9 percentile point gain in reading for second grade English Learner (EL) students over a two-year period. The national media listened—including major venues such as the *New York Times* and the *Washington Post*—and published prominent articles and op-ed pieces about Oceanside.

What made Oceanside so special for critics of bilingual education was

Kenji Hakuta, "Silence from Oceanside and the Future of Bilingual Education," www.stanford.edu/~hakuta, August 28, 2001. Copyright © 2001 by Kenji Hakuta. Reproduced by permission.

its superintendent, Ken Noonan, who gave eloquent testimony to the salvation bestowed upon his troubled district by Proposition 227. And he carried impeccable credentials. For one, he had Latino roots, and thus hailed from a group that is the widely recognized beneficiary of bilingual education programs. He also had began his career as an advocate for bilingual education, then reluctantly went along with the dismantling of bilingual education following the passage of Proposition 227. The fact that his district test scores improved caused in him an experience he likens to a religious conversion. He has since been going around the country as a spokesperson for similar initiatives in Arizona (which passed last year), New York, Texas, Massachusetts, and Colorado.

The test results for 2001 have just been released, . . . [and] the news from Oceanside for EL students is not good. The scores have stalled, and in some grade levels, they have even dropped. Third grade reading scores for EL students at Oceanside comes in at a national percentile score of 22, even below the statewide EL percentile score of 23. In 7 out of 12 schools, the reading scores dropped from 2000 to 2001, going against a statewide trend of rising scores.

Not surprisingly, there is silence on the website of Mr. Unz (www. onenation.org). From his perspective, it is embarassing news, and comes at a critical time in his campaign in several states, as well as at a key moment in the House-Senate conference committee on the education bill that includes bilingual education.

What went wrong at Oceanside? Actually, in my opinion, nothing. What was wrong to begin with was calling last year's [2000] Oceanside test results a miracle. Oceanside's test scores in 1998, the baseline year when California started testing its students using standardized tests, were far below statewide averages to start. For example in reading, Oceanside was at the 12th percentile compared to a statewide 19th percentile in 2nd grade, 9th percentile compared to 14th percentile statewide in 3rd grade. The remarkable gains in 1999 were accountable due to the old well-known statistical artifact, regression to the mean, in addition to the fact that the school system was getting accustomed to the test. Then the additional increase last year likely came about from something like an accounting trick. Oceanside kept a disproportionate number of high-scoring students in their pool of EL students, thereby increasing the average EL score. The real story of interest is that after three years, Oceanside finally managed to drag its test scores from rock bottom up to the statewide average for EL students. This is not a story about excellence, hardly a miracle.

## Bilingual education should be combined with other improvements in school

The lesson to be learned from Oceanside is that successfully educating EL students is hard and frustrating work, as Mr. Noonan must well know. Educators and researchers have been struggling with this for well over 30 years. Contrary to popular wisdom, systematic evaluations show bilingual education to be superior to English-only approaches in promoting English reading. But that advantage is fairly small if it is not combined with other costly efforts to improve the school conditions, including better facilities, visionary and sensitive school leadership, and instructional approaches that go far beyond the tired refrain of the language of instruction. The challenge is all the more daunting because all of this reform must take place in schools in highly stressed conditions—high poverty, low parent literacy and linguistically segregated. Such is the reality of why it is so difficult to mount effective programs to address the needs of EL students.

Unlike many of my friends from the advocacy community who believe that Mr. Unz has done nothing more than stir racist and xenophobic sentiment, I am of the opinion that his efforts have actually provided some valuable service to the plight of English Learners. By putting an initiative on the books, he has sharply focused public attention on the failure of existing school programs to bring them to high academic standards. This year's results from Oceanside furthermore demonstrate the difficulty and complexity of the job. The real damage that Mr. Unz has done is to offer a highly restrictive and ineffective alternative to the status quo, namely severe limits on bilingual education in spite of the evidence demonstrating its effectiveness.

> *Clearly, the lesson from Oceanside is the rejection of a Proposition 227–like rigid prescription for English immersion.*

What are the alternatives now for states facing Mr. Unz's initiatives, and for the nation contemplating the future of the federal role in bilingual education? Clearly, the lesson from Oceanside is the rejection of a Proposition 227–like rigid prescription for English immersion to the exclusion of bilingual education. But far more important is the encouragement of experimenting with a combination of systemic efforts that go far beyond the debate about the language of instruction. One should look seriously at the implications of a widely respected decision in 1981 by the US 5th Circuit Court in a decision, *Castañeda v. Pickard*, that laid down principles for what would be considered appropriate instructional practices for EL students. Such practices would be (1) based on sound educational research and theory; (2) implemented with adequate commitment and resources; (3) evaluated for effectiveness after a period of time; and (4) if it is not effective, the theory or implementation needs to be revisited. Regardless of whether a program is bilingual or English immersion, it would be prudent to use the principles of Castañeda to see how the program could be developed and modified in the service of effectiveness. Proposition 227 was never based on sound research, and while it gained national attention for why we should pay attention to the potential of immigrant students, it has not worked and should not become a national model. The Castañeda guidelines may sound like common sense, but offer a way of guiding rigorous evaluation of thoughtful programs within a legal framework, and furthermore show a way out of the conundrum of political advocacy endemic to the bilingual versus English-only debate.

# 10

# English Should Remain the Primary Language of the United States

## John Hewko

*John Hewko is an attorney and recently a visiting scholar at the Carnegie Endowment for International Peace.*

English is, and should be, the universal language of discourse in America. Immigrants are better served if they learn English from the moment they start attending school. That was the way earlier immigrants learned English, and it helped them prosper. Bilingual education will not help immigrants assimilate into American society. It is bad policy for the United States and for its immigrants and should be discarded. However, learning English does not mean that one forsakes one's native language. English can be the language in school, and the native language the language at home and in church.

Whether we like it or not, the universal language of discourse in America is and should be English. I speak from experience. My parents were immigrants and my wife is an immigrant from Argentina. I speak six languages and have spent 15 of the past 20 years living and working abroad. Bilingual education is bad policy for the United States and for its immigrants and should be discarded, once and for all, as a failed and misguided idea.

My parents came to this country from Ukraine after World War II. My father was 19, my mother 11. They spoke no English when they arrived. Today, my father's English is perfect, although when he says words such as "European" or "worm" you can tell that he was not born in Detroit. My mother sounds like any other born and raised Midwesterner. Why? Because when they arrived they had no choice but to learn English—and learn it quickly.

John Hewko, "Keep the U.S. English Speaking," *Christian Science Monitor*, vol. 95, December 3, 2002, p. 9. Copyright © 2002 by John Hewko. Reproduced by permission.

## The importance of assimilation

I have no doubt that my mother's first year in a Catholic school must have been intimidating and difficult, and my father must have complained as he slogged through his university texts, translating them from English into German and then into Ukrainian because there were no good English-Ukrainian technical dictionaries available. But then again, no one forced them to come to the United States. Sure, signs, government forms, ballots, television, phone recordings, and school instruction in Ukrainian would have helped. But this approach would have only served to slow considerably their integration into American society, their ability to benefit from higher education, and to advance in their chosen professions.

I never once heard my parents (or my grandparents for that matter) complain about their fate. It was simply accepted that when one decided to come to the United States, the priority was to learn English—a message quite clearly reinforced by society at that time.

But times have changed. Voters in Colorado failed to pass an initiative this fall [2000] that would enforce English-only education programs. Meanwhile, 60 percent of the voters in Massachusetts passed a measure to get rid of bilingual education. Sadly, the electorate in Colorado has missed the boat.

---

*It was simply accepted that when one decided to come to the United States, the priority was to learn English.*

---

Being thrown into an English-speaking world without a bilingual education parachute didn't mean that my parents left their Ukrainian heritage behind or failed to pass it along to us children. At home and at church, we spoke Ukrainian and each Saturday my siblings and I were sent to a school organized and financed by the Ukrainian community in Detroit where we studied Ukrainian language, history, and culture. I went to kindergarten knowing very little English. However, by the end of the year, my parents found they were fighting an increasingly losing battle to keep me from speaking only English. A balance was struck. On public time, my world was English speaking. During the weekends and at home, it was Ukrainian. The system worked. And we became full-fledged English-speaking Americans without sacrificing our ancestral heritage.

## English immersion is compatible with diversity

The same can be said of my daughter Maria. She was born nine years ago when we were living in Kiev, Ukraine. When she was 4, we moved to the Czech Republic. Since at the time we spoke Spanish and Ukrainian at home, she went to the International School in Prague knowing almost no English. In fact, of her 19 classmates from almost a dozen countries, almost all spoke little or no English. But by the end of the year, these school-children—living in Prague and using Dutch, Swedish, German, or Georgian at home—could have passed for any American kid. One can only wonder how long they would have needed to learn English had bilingual education been the official philosophy at the International School in Prague.

That is not to say that Americans should not speak or learn other languages and that the rich cultural diversity of America should not be preserved.

---

*We became full-fledged English-speaking Americans without sacrificing our ancestral heritage.*

---

However, we should not confuse an English-speaking country whose citizens also happen to speak other languages and maintain different cultural traditions with a bilingual society.

History is full of examples of societies being torn apart by linguistic differences and it would be a needless shame were the same to occur here. My generation, and countless generations of immigrants, was exposed to a system that encouraged assimilation and did not consider it to be a negative.

English can be learned without destroying diversity. It is a system that has worked, will continue to work, and should never have been abandoned in the first place.

# 11

# Americans Should Not Fear Language Diversity

## Robert D. King

*Robert D. King holds the Audre and Bernard Rapoport Chair of Jewish Studies at the University of Texas at Austin, where he teaches and writes about linguistics, India, and the Yiddish language. His latest book is* Nehru and the Language Politics of India.

The issue of language is not about to tear apart American society, despite the warnings of groups that believe otherwise and are actively pushing legislation that would make English the official national language. The English-only movement faces tough odds. Whereas in much of the rest of the world language defines ethnic and national identity, in the United States Americans are united by many other traditions, including respect for the individual, equality of opportunity, and a history of freedom and valor. Rather than fearing language diversity, Americans should celebrate their country's linguistic richness.

We have known race riots, draft riots, labor violence, secession, antiwar protests, and a whiskey rebellion, but one kind of trouble we've never had: a language riot. Language riot? It sounds like a joke. The very idea of language as a political force—as something that might threaten to split a country wide apart—is alien to our way of thinking and to our cultural traditions.

This may be changing. . . . [In 1996] the U.S. House of Representatives approved a bill that would make English the official language of the United States. The vote was 259 to 169, with 223 Republicans and thirty-six Democrats voting in favor and eight Republicans, 160 Democrats, and one independent voting against. The debate was intense, acrid, and partisan. [Editor's note: As of March 2003, no federal English-only legislation has become law.] On March 25 [1996], the Supreme Court agreed to review a case involving an Arizona law that would require public employees to conduct government business only in English. Arizona is one of several states that have passed "Official English" or "English Only" laws.

Robert D. King, "Should English Be the Law?" *The Atlantic Monthly*, vol. 279, April 1997, pp. 55–64.

The appeal to the Supreme Court followed a 6-to-5 ruling, in October of 1995, by a federal appeals court striking down the Arizona law. [In January 1999, the Supreme Court refused to revive Arizona's English-only law.] These events suggest how divisive a public issue language could become in America—even if it has until now scarcely been taken seriously.

Traditionally, the American way has been to make English the national language—but to do so quietly, locally, without fuss. The Constitution is silent on language: the Founding Fathers had no need to legislate that English be the official language of the country. It has always been taken for granted that English is the national language, and that one must learn English in order to make it in America.

> *The . . . idea of language as . . . something that might threaten to split a country wide apart . . . is alien to our way of thinking and to our cultural traditions.*

To say that language has never been a major force in American history or politics, however, is not to say that politicians have always resisted linguistic jingoism. In 1753 Benjamin Franklin voiced his concern that German immigrants were not learning English: "Those [Germans] who come hither are generally the most ignorant Stupid Sort of their own Nation. . . . they will soon so out number us, that all the advantages we have will not, in My Opinion, be able to preserve our language, and even our government will become precarious." Theodore Roosevelt articulated the unspoken American linguistic-melting-pot theory when he boomed, "We have room for but one language here, and that is the English language, for we intend to see that the crucible turns our people out as Americans, of American nationality, and not as dwellers in a polyglot boarding house." And: "We must have but one flag. We must also have but one language. That must be the language of the Declaration of Independence, of Washington's Farewell address, of Lincoln's Gettysburg speech and second inaugural."

## The English-only movement

. . . [Roosevelt's] linguistic tub-thumping long typified the tradition of American politics. That tradition began to change in the wake of the anything-goes attitudes and the celebration of cultural differences arising in the 1960s. A 1975 amendment to the Voting Rights Act of 1965 mandated the "bilingual ballot" under certain circumstances, notably when the voters of selected language groups reached five percent or more in a voting district. Bilingual education became a byword of educational thinking during the 1960s. By the 1970s linguists had demonstrated convincingly—at least to other academics—that black English (today called African-American vernacular English or Ebonics) was not "bad" English but a different kind of authentic English with its own rules. Predictably, there have been scattered demands that black English be included in bilingual-education programs.

It was against this background that the movement to make English the official language of the country arose. In 1981 Senator S. I. Hayakawa, long a leading critic of bilingual education and bilingual ballots, introduced in the U.S. Senate a constitutional amendment that not only would have made English the official language but would have prohibited federal and state laws and regulations requiring the use of other languages. His English Language Amendment died in the Ninety-seventh Congress.

In 1983 the organization called U.S. English was founded by Hayakawa and John Tanton, a Michigan ophthalmologist. The primary purpose of the organization was to promote English as the official language of the United States. . . . Official English initiatives were passed by California in 1986, by Arkansas, Mississippi, North Carolina, North Dakota, and South Carolina in 1987, by Colorado, Florida, and Arizona in 1988, and by Alabama in 1990. The majorities voting for these initiatives were generally not insubstantial: California's, for example, passed by 73 percent.

## Conservatives and liberals

It was probably inevitable that the Official English (or English Only—the two names are used almost interchangeably) movement would acquire a conservative, almost reactionary undertone in the 1990s. Official English is politically very incorrect. But its cofounder John Tanton brought with him strong liberal credentials. He had been active in the Sierra Club and Planned Parenthood, and in the 1970s served as the national president of Zero Population Growth. Early advisers of U.S. English resist ideological pigeonholing: they included Walter Annenberg, Jacques Barzun, Bruno Bettelheim, Alistair Cooke, Denton Cooley, Walter Cronkite, Angier Biddle Duke, George Gilder, Sidney Hook, Norman Podhoretz, Arnold Schwarzenegger, and Karl Shapiro. In 1987 U.S. English installed as its president Linda Chávez, a Hispanic who had been prominent in the Reagan Administration. A year later she resigned her position, citing "repugnant" and "anti-Hispanic" overtones in an internal memorandum written by Tanton. Tanton, too, resigned, and Walter Cronkite, describing the affair as "embarrassing," left the advisory board. One board member, Norman Cousins, defected in 1986, alluding to the "negative symbolic significance" of California's Official English initiative, Proposition 63. . . .

The popular wisdom is that conservatives are pro and liberals con. True, conservatives such as George Will and William F. Buckley Jr. have written columns supporting Official English. But would anyone characterize as conservatives the present and past U.S. English board members Alistair Cooke, Walter Cronkite, and Norman Cousins? One of the strongest opponents of bilingual education is the Mexican-American writer Richard Rodríguez, best known for his eloquent autobiography, *Hunger of Memory* (1982). There is a strain of American liberalism that defines itself in nostalgic devotion to the melting pot.

For several years relevant bills awaited consideration in the U.S. House of Representatives. The Emerson Bill (H.R. 123), passed by the House . . . [in August 1996], specifies English as the official language of government, and requires that the government "preserve and enhance" the official status of English. Exceptions are made for the teaching of foreign languages;

for actions necessary for public health, international relations, foreign trade, and the protection of the rights of criminal defendants; and for the use of "terms of art" from languages other than English . . .

What are the chances that some version of Official English will become federal law? Any language bill will face tough odds in the Senate, because some western senators have opposed English Only measures in the past for various reasons, among them a desire by Republicans not to alienate the growing number of Hispanic Republicans, most of whom are uncomfortable with mandated monolingualism. Texas Governor George W. Bush, too, has forthrightly said that he would oppose any English Only proposals in his state. Several of the Republican candidates for President in 1996 (an interesting exception is Phil Gramm) endorsed versions of Official English, as has Newt Gingrich. While governor of Arkansas [1978–1982], Bill Clinton signed into law an English Only bill. As President [1993–2001], he has described his earlier action as a mistake.

Many issues intersect in the controversy over Official English: immigration (above all), the rights of minorities (Spanish-speaking minorities in particular), the pros and cons of bilingual education, tolerance, how best to educate the children of immigrants, and the place of cultural diversity in school curricula and in American society in general. The question that lies at the root of most of the uneasiness is this: Is America threatened by the preservation of languages other than English? Will America, if it continues on its traditional path of benign linguistic neglect, go the way of Belgium, Canada, and Sri Lanka—three countries among many whose unity is gravely imperiled by language and ethnic conflicts?. . .

## An explosive issue in other countries

In much of the world, ethnic unity and cultural identification are routinely defined by language. To be Arab is to speak Arabic. Bengali identity is based on language in spite of the division of Bengali-speakers between Hindu India and Muslim Bangladesh. When eastern Pakistan seceded from greater Pakistan in 1971, it named itself Bangladesh: *desa* means "country"; *bangla* means not the Bengali people or the Bengali territory but the Bengali language.

---

*America may be threatened by immigration. . . . But America is not threatened by language.*

---

Scratch most nationalist movements and you find a linguistic grievance. The demands for independence of the Baltic states (Latvia, Lithuania, and Estonia) were intimately bound up with fears for the loss of their respective languages and cultures in a sea of Russianness. In Belgium the war between French and Flemish threatens an already weakly fused country. The present atmosphere of Belgium is dark and anxious, costive; the metaphor of divorce is a staple of private and public discourse. The lines of terrorism in Sri Lanka are drawn between Tamil Hindus and Sinhalese Buddhists—and also between the Tamil and Sinhalese languages. Worship of the French language fortifies the movement for an independent

Quebec. Whether a united Canada will survive into the twenty-first century is a question too close to call. Much of the anxiety about language in the United States is probably fueled by the "Quebec problem": unlike Belgium, which is a small European country, or Sri Lanka, which is halfway around the world, Canada is our close neighbor.

Language is a convenient surrogate for nonlinguistic claims that are often awkward to articulate, for they amount to a demand for more political and economic power. Militant Sikhs in India call for a state of their own: Khalistan ("Land of the Pure" in Punjabi). They frequently couch this as a demand for a linguistic state, which has a certain simplicity about it, a clarity of motive—justice, even, because states in India are normally linguistic states. But the Sikh demands blend religion, economics, language, and retribution for sins both punished and unpunished in a country where old sins cast long shadows.

Language is an explosive issue in the countries of the former Soviet Union. The language conflict in Estonia has been especially bitter. Ethnic Russians make up almost a third of Estonia's population, and most of them do not speak or read Estonian, although Russians have lived in Estonia for more than a generation. Estonia has passed legislation requiring knowledge of the Estonian language as a condition of citizenship. Nationalist groups in independent Lithuania sought restrictions on the use of Polish—again, old sins, long shadows. . . .

## Hope for language tolerance

Is there no hope for language tolerance? Some countries manage to maintain their unity in the face of multilingualism. Examples are Finland, with a Swedish minority, and a number of African and Southeast Asian countries. Two others could not be more unlike as countries go: Switzerland and India.

German, French, Italian, and Romansh are the languages of Switzerland. The first three can be and are used for official purposes; all four are designated "national" languages. Switzerland is politically almost hyperstable. It has language problems (Romansh is losing ground), but they are not major, and they are never allowed to threaten national unity.

Contrary to public perception, India gets along pretty well with a host of different languages. The Indian constitution officially recognizes nineteen languages, English among them. Hindi is specified in the constitution as the national language of India, but that is a pious postcolonial fiction: outside the Hindi-speaking northern heartland of India, people don't want to learn it. English functions more nearly than Hindi as India's lingua franca.

From 1947, when India obtained its independence from the British, until the 1960s blood ran in the streets and people died because of language. Hindi absolutists wanted to force Hindi on the entire country, which would have split India between north and south and opened up other fracture lines as well. For as long as possible Jawaharlal Nehru, independent India's first Prime Minister, resisted nationalist demands to redraw the capricious state boundaries of British India according to language. By the time he capitulated, the country had gained a precious decade to prove its viability as a union.

Why is it that India preserves its unity with not just two languages to contend with, as Belgium, Canada, and Sri Lanka have, but nineteen? The answer is that India, like Switzerland, has a strong national identity. The two countries share something big and almost mystical that holds each together in a union transcending language. That something I call "unique otherness."

> *We are not even close to the danger point. I suggest that we relax and luxuriate in our linguistic richness and our traditional tolerance of language differences.*

The Swiss have what the political scientist Karl Deutsch called "learned habits, preferences, symbols, memories, and patterns of land-holding": customs, cultural traditions, and political institutions that bind them closer to one another than to people of France, Germany, or Italy living just across the border and speaking the same language. There is Switzerland's traditional neutrality, its system of universal military training (the "citizen army"), its consensual allegiance to a strong Swiss franc—and fondue, yodeling, skiing, and mountains. Set against all this, the fact that Switzerland has four languages doesn't even approach the threshold of becoming a threat.

As for India, what Vincent Smith, in the *Oxford History of India*, calls its "deep underlying fundamental unity" resides in institutions and beliefs such as caste, cow worship, sacred places, and much more. Consider *dharma, karma,* and *maya,* the three root convictions of Hinduism; India's historical epics; Gandhi; *ahimsa* (nonviolence); vegetarianism; a distinctive cuisine and way of eating; marriage customs; a shared past; and what the Indologist Ainslie Embree calls "Brahmanical ideology." In other words, "We are Indian; we are different."

Belgium and Canada have never managed to forge a stable national identity; Czechoslovakia and Yugoslavia never did either. Unique otherness immunizes countries against linguistic destabilization. Even Switzerland and especially India have problems; in any country with as many different languages as India has, language will never not be a problem. However, it is one thing to have a major illness with a bleak prognosis; it is another to have a condition that is irritating and occasionally painful but not life-threatening.

## Laws do not change language attitudes

History teaches a plain lesson about language and governments: there is almost nothing the government of a free country can do to change language usage and practice significantly, to force its citizens to use certain languages in preference to others, and to discourage people from speaking a language they wish to continue to speak. (The rebirth of Hebrew in Palestine and Israel's successful mandate that Hebrew be spoken and written by Israelis is a unique event in the annals of language history.) Quebec has since the 1970s passed an array of laws giving French a virtual monopoly in the province. One consequence—unintended, one wishes to believe—of these laws is that last year kosher products imported for Passover were kept off the shelves, because the packages were not labeled in French. Wise governments keep their hands off language to the extent that it is politically possible to do so.

We like to believe that to pass a law is to change behavior; but passing laws about language, in a free society, almost never changes attitudes or behavior. Gaelic (Irish) is living out a slow, inexorable decline in Ireland despite enormous government support of every possible kind since Ireland gained its independence from Britain. The Welsh language, in contrast, is alive today in Wales in spite of heavy discrimination during its history. Three out of four people in the northern and western counties of Gwynedd and Dyfed speak Welsh.

I said earlier that language is a convenient surrogate for other national problems. Official English obviously has a lot to do with concern about immigration, perhaps especially Hispanic immigration. America may be threatened by immigration; I don't know. But America is not threatened by language.

## Americans have other symbols

The usual arguments made by academics against Official English are commonsensical. Who needs a law when, according to the 1990 census, 94 percent of American residents speak English anyway? (Mauro E. Mujica, the chairman of U.S. English, cites a higher figure: 97 percent.) Not many of today's immigrants will see their first language survive into the second generation. This is in fact the common lament of first-generation immigrants: their children are not learning their language and are losing the culture of their parents. Spanish is hardly a threat to English, in spite of isolated (and easily visible) cases such as Miami, New York City, and pockets of the Southwest and southern California. The everyday language of south Texas is Spanish, and yet south Texas is not about to secede from America.

But empirical, calm arguments don't engage the real issue: language is a symbol, an icon. Nobody who favors a constitutional ban against flag burning will ever be persuaded by the argument that the flag is, after all, just a "piece of cloth." A draft card in the 1960s was never merely a piece of paper. Neither is a marriage license.

Language, as one linguist has said, is "not primarily a means of communication but a means of communion." Romanticism exalted language, made it mystical, sublime—a bond of national identity. At the same time, Romanticism created a monster: it made of language a means for destroying a country.

America has that unique otherness of which I spoke. In spite of all our racial divisions and economic unfairness, we have the frontier tradition, respect for the individual, and opportunity; we have our love affair with the automobile; we have in our history a civil war that freed the slaves and was fought with valor; and we have sports, hot dogs, hamburgers, and milk shakes—things big and small, noble and petty, important and trifling. "We are Americans; we are different."

If I'm wrong, then the great American experiment will fail—not because of language but because it no longer means anything to be an American; because we have forfeited that "willingness of the heart" that

F. Scott Fitzgerald wrote was America; because we are no longer joined by Lincoln's "mystic chords of memory."

We are not even close to the danger point. I suggest that we relax and luxuriate in our linguistic richness and our traditional tolerance of language differences. Language does not threaten American unity. Benign neglect is a good policy for any country when it comes to language, and it's a good policy for America.

# Organizations to Contact

The editors have compiled the following list of organizations concerned with the issues debated in this book. The descriptions are derived from materials provided by the organizations. All have publications or information available for interested readers. The list was compiled on the date of publication of the present volume; the information provided here may change. Be aware that many organizations take several weeks or longer to respond to inquiries, so allow as much time as possible.

**California Association for Bilingual Education (CABE)**
16033 E. San Bernardino Rd., Covina, CA 91722-3900
(626) 814-4441 • fax: (626) 814-4640
e-mail: info@bilingualeducation.org • website: www.bilingualeducation.org

CABE promotes excellence in bilingual education, equal educational opportunities for all, and an understanding of the linguistic and cultural needs of language-minority groups. It implements educational projects that develop the competence of parents, educators, administrators, community leaders, and policymakers. It also conducts research and development on bilingual education. The association has published books on language, including *Language, Power, and Identity; Reclaiming Our Voices*; and *Negotiating Identities*.

**Center for Applied Linguistics (CAL)**
4646 Fortieth St. NW, Washington, DC 20016-1859
(202) 362-0700 • fax: (202) 362-3740
e-mail: info@cal.org • website: www.cal.org

CAL assists schools and educators in developing effective language programs by offering professional development for the teaching of foreign languages and the teaching of English as a second language (ESL) and a foreign language. It also evaluates bilingual, ESL, and foreign language programs and offers technical assistance in solving language-related problems. The center disseminates information through clearinghouses, databases, directories, print and on-line publications, research reports, educational practice reports, teacher guides, and videos. Its more recent publications include the report "Adult English Language Learners" and the brochure "Why Start and Maintain an SNS Program."

**Center for Equal Opportunity (CEO)**
14 Pidgeon Hill Dr., Suite 500, Sterling, VA 20165
(703) 421-5443 • fax: (703) 421-6401
e-mail: comment@ceousa.org • website: www.ceousa.org

The CEO is a research and policy organization that promotes equal opportunity and racial harmony by supporting policies that it considers "colorblind." One of its goals is to block or recall race-conscious public policies. Its publications include studies on English language and acquisition, racial and ethnic preferences in schools, immigration and assimilation, and multicultural education. It also publishes teachers' guides on English immersion.

**Education Resources Information Center (ERIC)**
Digests on Bilingualism and Bilingual Education
2277 Research Blvd., MS 6M, Rockville, MD 20850
(800) LET-ERIC • (800) 538-3742
e-mail: accesseric@accesseric.org • website: www.eric.ed.gov

ERIC is a national information system that provides access to an extensive body of literature on education. Supported by the U.S. Department of Education, it maintains a database of more than 1 million records of journal articles, research reports, curriculum and teaching guides, conference papers, and books. It also provides research syntheses, electronic journals, on-line directories, and reference and referral services on various aspects of education.

**English First**
8001 Forbes Pl., Suite 109, Springfield, VA 22151
(703) 321-8818 • fax: (703) 321-8408
e-mail: webmaster@englishfirst.org • website: www.englishfirst.org

English First, founded in 1986, is a national lobby organization that seeks to make English the official language of the United States, to give every child the chance to learn English, and to eliminate multilingual policies. It is active in influencing policymaking at the state and federal levels. One of its current projects is the repeal of Executive Order 13166, which ensures the language rights of minority groups. The organization's website contains a media archive, updates on bilingual education and English immersion, and the organization's current legislation campaigns.

**English for the Children Initiative**
555 Bryant St., #371, Palo Alto, CA 94301
(650) 853-0365 • fax: (650) 853-0362
website: www.onenation.org

English for the Children Initiative is an advocacy group founded by businessman Ron Unz, who launched Proposition 227 in California in 1997. The organization seeks to replace bilingual education with English immersion throughout the country. The organization's website contains a media archive on bilingual education and English immersion, Unz's writings, a list of the organization's ongoing ballot initiatives, and contact names and addresses for ongoing campaigns.

**Institute for Research in English Acquisition and Development (READ)**
14 Pidgeon Hill Dr., Suite 500, Sterling, VA 20165
(703) 421-5443 • fax: (703) 421-6401
e-mail: comment@ceousa.org • website: www.ceousa.org

READ supports research on English language learning and effective schooling for language-minority children. One of its goals is the reform of bilingual education. It assists school districts in developing and evaluating programs for limited-English students. It also provides information to scholars, educators, policymakers, and the general public. Its publications include research reports on effective educational programs for English-limited students and the annual journal *READ Perspectives*. The institute also distributes books, including *The Politics of Bilingual Education, The Unmasking of Americans: How Multiculturalism Has Undermined the Assimilation Ethic,* and *Losing Our Language: How Multicultural Classroom Instruction Is Undermining Our Children's Ability to Read, Write, and Reason.*

**Language Policy Research Unit (LPRU)**
College of Education, Arizona State University
e-mail: LPRUlist@asu.edu • website: www.asu.edu

The LPRU is a research and policy organization that studies the challenges and opportunities of national and global multilingualism. It conducts various studies to promote equitable language policies, including demographic studies and their implications on language rights and preservation, as well as language conflicts and minority language accommodation and promotion. Its publications include research reports, policy briefs, a news archive on language policy, and the *Journal of Language, Identity, and Education*.

**National Association for Bilingual Education (NABE)**
1030 Fifteenth St. NW, Suite 470, Washington, DC 20005
(202) 898-1829 • fax: (202) 789-2866
website: www.nabe.org

NABE seeks to provide language-minority children access to high-quality educational programs and opportunities that will help them achieve bilingualism and biliteracy. It advocates policies favorable to bilingual education, conducts fund-raising, holds conferences for teachers and school administrators, and publishes various publications, including brochures, the magazine *News*, and the *Bilingual Research Journal*.

**National Clearinghouse for English Language Acquisition and Language Instruction Educational Programs (NCELA)**
2121 K St. NW, Suite 260, Washington, DC 20037
toll free: (800) 321-6223 • (202) 467-0867 • fax: (800) 531-9347
e-mail: askncela@ncela.gwu.edu • website: www.ncela.gwu.edu

Formerly known as the National Clearinghouse for Bilingual Education, the NCELA, an organization funded by the Department of Education, collects, analyzes, and disseminates information on the effective education of linguistically and culturally diverse learners in the United States. It helps school districts develop programs and implement strategies to help all students achieve high academic standards. Its publications include research reports, monographs, guides on bilingual-education models, parents' guides, teacher resource guides, policy reports, and symposia proceedings. The clearinghouse maintains a website that features a wealth of information resources, the news bulletin *Newsline*, and the monthly electronic magazine *Outlook*. It also conducts conferences for teachers and administrators.

**National Council of La Raza (NCLR)**
1111 Nineteenth NW, Suite 1000, Washington, DC 20003
(202) 785-1670
website: www.nclr.org

The NCLR, a private nonprofit organization that seeks to improve opportunities for Hispanic Americans, has education as one of its concerns. It supports community-based organizations in the areas of management, governance, program operations, and resource development. It also carries out research, policy analysis, and advocacy, including providing a Hispanic perspective on issues such as education, immigration, health, employment, and civil rights. Its publications include policy papers; briefs on government policies; fact sheets on income, poverty, and welfare reform; and research reports.

**Southwest Center for Educational Equity and Language Diversity (SCEED)**
College of Education, Arizona State University, PO Box 871511, Tempe, Arizona 85287-1511
(480) 965-7134 • fax: (480) 965-5164
e-mail: josue@asu.edu • website: www.asu.edu

The organization develops educational programs that help meet the needs of the multicultural region it serves—the Southwestern borderlands. It disseminates information on current research and policy issues on language diversity and educational equity that affect schools and communities. It also develops and implements educational programs that improve the education of immigrant children, with special emphasis on the Latino population. Together with NABE, it publishes the *Bilingual Research Journal*.

**U.S. English Foundation**
1747 Pennsylvania Ave. NW, Suite 1050, Washington, DC 20006
(202) 833-0100
e-mail: info@us-english.org • website: www.us-english.org

The foundation's mission is to ensure that English continues to be the mainstream language in America, providing a unifying force among ethnic groups. It helps immigrants learn English by providing grants to volunteer organizations that teach adult English classes and scholarships in postgraduate English-language education. It also maintains a legal defense fund that represents official English advocates in court, and it disseminates information on methods in teaching English.

**U.S. English Incorporated**
1747 Pennsylvania Ave. NW, Suite 1050, Washington, DC 20006
(202) 833-0100
e-mail: info@us-english.org • website: www.us-english.org

U.S. English Incorporated, a sister organization of the U.S. English Foundation, is a lobby organization that promotes English as the official language of the country. It claims to be the oldest and largest citizens' action group with 1.7 million members. The organization promotes its goal through signature campaigns, media support, and legislative action at the state and federal levels.

# Bibliography

## Books

| | |
|---|---|
| Colin Baker | *Foundations of Bilingual Education and Bilingualism.* Clevedon, England: Multilingual Matters, 2001. |
| Abdul Karim Bangura and Martin C. Muo | *United States Congress and Bilingual Education.* New York: Peter Lang, 2001. |
| Ellen Bialystok | *Bilingualism in Development: Language, Literacy, and Cognition.* New York: Cambridge University Press, 2001. |
| Maria Estela Brisk | *Bilingual Education: From Compensatory to Quality Schooling.* Mahwah, NJ: Lawrence Erlbaum Associates, 1998. |
| James Crawford | *At War with Diversity: U.S. Language Policy in an Age of Anxiety.* Clevedon, England: Multilingual Matters, 2000. |
| James Crawford | *Bilingual Education: History, Politics, Theory, and Practice.* Los Angeles: Bilingual Educational Services, 1991. |
| James Crawford | *Hold Your Tongue: Bilingualism and the Politics of "English Only."* Menlo Park, CA: Addison-Wesley, 1992. |
| Jim Cummins | *Language, Power, and Pedagogy: Bilingual Children in the Crossfire.* Clevedon, England: Multilingual Matters, 2000. |
| Majula Datta, ed. | *Bilinguality and Literacy: Principles and Practice.* New York: Continuum, 2000. |
| Peter Duignan | *Bilingual Education.* Stanford: Hoover Institution Press, 1998. |
| Kenji Hakuta and Diane August, eds. | *Educating Language Minority Children.* Washington, DC: National Academy, 1998. |
| Stephen Krashen | *Under Attack: The Case Against Bilingual Education.* Culver City, CA: Language Education Associates, 1996. |
| Paul Lang | *The English Language Debate: One Nation, One Language.* Springfield, NJ: Enslow, 1995. |
| Arnold H. Leibowitz | *The Bilingual Education Act: A Legislative Analysis.* Rosslyn, VA: Inter-America Research Associates, 1980. |
| Christina Bratt Paulston | *Bilingual Education: Theories and Issues.* Rowley, MA: Newbury House, 1980. |
| Rosalie Pedalino Porter | *Forked Tongue: The Politics of Bilingual Education.* New York: BasicBooks, 1990. |
| Lucy Tse | *Why Don't They Learn English: Separating Fact from Fallacy in the U.S. Language Debate.* New York: Teachers College Press, 2001. |

## Periodicals

George Amselle — "Bye-Bye to Bilingual Ed?" *World & I*, March 2000.

Michael Barone — "In Plain English," *U.S. News & World Report*, May 29, 2000.

William F. Buckley Jr. — "On the Right: W.'s Strange Flirtation," *National Review*, August 20, 2001.

*Economist* — "A Raw Deal," March 11, 2000.

Siobhan Gorman — "California's Language Wars, Part II," *National Journal*, July 31, 1999.

Scott S. Greenberger — "Bilingual Education Loses Favor with Some Educators," *Boston Globe*, August 5, 2001.

John Hewko — "Keep the U.S. English Speaking," *The Christian Science Monitor*," December 3, 2002.

Kristin L. Johannsen — "Bridging the Gap: Learning Languages Has Taken a Quantum Leap As It Enters the Twenty-First Century," *World & I*, September 2001.

Susan Katz — "Banishing Bilingualism," *Nation*, December 9, 2002.

Alana Keynes — "California Anti-Bilingual Education Law Upheld by Appeals Court," *Education Daily*, October 9, 2002.

*Newsweek* — "Habla Ingles, Por Favor," March 12, 2001.

Ken Noonan — "I Believed that Bilingual Education Was the Best . . . Until the Kids Proved Me Wrong," *The Washington Post*, September 3, 2000.

Geoffrey Nunberg — "Lingo Jingo: English Only and the New Nativism," *American Prospect*, July/August 1997.

Andrew Phillips — "The English-Only Debate," *Maclean's*, May 5, 1997.

Rosalie Pedalino Porter — "The Case Against Bilingualism," *Atlantic Monthly*, May 1998.

Rosalie Pedalino Porter — "Porter Challenges Bilingual Education," *Insight on the News*, September 10, 2001.

Richard Rothstein — "Bilingualism: The Controversy," *Phi Delta Kappan*, May 1998.

Wayne P. Thomas and Virginia P. Collier — "Two Languages are Better than One," *Educational Leadership*, December 1997.

Anand Vaishnav — "California Bilingual Reform Has Pros, Cons," *Boston Globe*, October 27, 2002.

Kathleen Wilson and Jean Cowden Moore — "English Immersion Gets Good Grades," *Ventura County Star*, May 1, 2002.

## Internet Sources

Jim Boulet Jr. — "Win Some, Lose Some," *National Review Online*, November 7, 2002. www.nationalreview.com.

James Crawford    "Proposition 227 Failed 1,393,849 Children in 2001," James Crawford's Language Policy Website and Emporium, November 1998. http://ourworld.compuserve.com.

Kenji Hakuta    "Silence from Oceanside and the Future of Bilingual Education," Kenji's Homepage, Stanford University. August 18, 2001. www.stanford.edu/~hakuta.

Robert D. King    "Should English be the Law?" *The Atlantic Online*, April 1997. www.theatlantic.com.

Stephen Krashen    "Why Bilingual Education?" *ERIC Digests*. www.ericfacility.net.

Jill Kerper Mora    "Debunking English-Only Ideology: Bilingual Educators are not the Enemy," San Diego State University, California, October 23, 2002. www.coe.sdsu.edu/people.

Jennifer Evelyn Orr et al.    "What Can We Learn About the Impact of Proposition 227," August 15, 2000. www.stanford.edu.

Ron C. Unz    "Bilingual Education Ineffective Initiative: Schools Harm Spanish-Speaking Kids by Not Teaching English," January 16, 1998. www.gseis.ucla.edu.

Mary Ann Zehr    "Early Bilingual Programs Found to Boost Test Scores," *Education Week Online*, September 4, 2002. www.edweek.org.

# Index